CAREERS in Child Care

Alma Lerner Visser
with
Patricia A. Woy

BETTERWAY PUBLICATIONS, INC.
WHITE HALL, VIRGINIA

Published by Betterway Publications, Inc.
P.O. Box 219
Crozet, VA 22932
(804) 823-5661

Cover design by Rick Britton
Typography by Park Lane Associates

Copyright © 1991 by Alma Lerner Visser and Patricia A. Woy
All rights reserved. No part of this book may be reproduced by any means, except by a reviewer who wishes to quote brief excerpts in connection with a review in a magazine or newspaper.

Library of Congress Cataloging-in-Publication Data
Visser, Alma Lerner
    Careers in child care / Alma Lerner Visser with Patricia A. Woy.
      p. cm.
    Includes bibliographical references and index.
    ISBN 1-55870-205-9 (pbk.) : $7.95
    1. Child care--Vocational guidance--United States. I. Woy,
Patricia A. II. Title.
HQ778.7.U6V59 1991
649'.1'02373--dc20   91-4073
                                                                                    CIP

Printed in the United States of America
0 9 8 7 6 5 4 3 2 1

To my number one supporter, Teunis, and to my beautiful grandchildren—Bradley, Benjamin, Brittany, Kira, Tracy, and Seth.

Acknowledgments

While the idea for this book came about during my child care career workshops, the book itself would never have gotten published without the help of child care staff across the nation, my associates, and my friends. I experienced warmth and kindness from each and every professional as they shared with me insight into their programs and services.

In my eyes, child care professionals are a special group of people who are dedicated to their cause. They are, indeed, endeared to my heart. I graciously thank the following people for their assistance:

Barbara Berg	Eileen Bornsheaur
Bette Koerner	Joanna Jones
Jean Cohn	Beverly Benjamin
Dennis Hudson	Bill Ewing
Judy Sanders	Judy Thomson
Cynthia Tyler	

Foreword

At last, we have a book that offers everything an aspiring child care worker needs to know about entering the field. The book's comprehensive reporting of jobs emphasizes the importance of caring for our nation's children in a quality child care setting. This book is also a "must" for parents who wish to acquaint themselves with quality day care criteria and child care issues.

Early childhood education has reached such a crisis that our United States lawmakers are finally focusing on funding programs. If we are going to provide quality education that addresses the needs of working parents, our overworked and underpaid child care providers must be taken seriously. *Careers in Child Care* addresses these issues.

The author's personal integrity shines through as she shares her concerns and experiences as one of the outstanding early childhood educators in Pomona Valley, California. If I can't answer one of my student's questions, I say, "Call Alma, she'll know." If she doesn't, you can be sure the question will be researched for the answer.

Joanna Jones, Ph.D.
Child Development Coordinator
Chaffey College, California

Contents

Introduction 9

SECTION I: EXPLORING CHILD CARE CAREERS

1. Understanding the Child Development Field 13
2. Goal Setting and Training Programs......................... 21
3. Techniques for Job-Seeking Success 29
4. Private Sector Careers 37
5. Public Sector Jobs.. 51
6. Other Potential Job Opportunities 59
7. Child Care Resource & Referral Agencies................. 69
8. Family Day Care 81
9. Child Care Center.. 91
10. New Century Careers 103
11. Role of the Child Care Advocate............................. 117

SECTION II: WORKING WITH CHILDREN AND FAMILIES

12. Curriculum Guide for Caregivers............................ 123
13. Multicultural, Anti-Bias Curriculum....................... 139
14. Guidance and Discipline... 143

APPENDICES

1. Professional Organizations and Advocacy Groups.... 151
2. Journals, Newsletters, and Periodicals 157
   Glossary 161
   Suggested Reading... 165
   Bibliography 167

   Index 169

Introduction

Recognizing the lack of up-to-date material in the ever-changing field of child care, the authors have written this book with you in mind. We believe that the more knowledge you have about child development and career options, the easier it will be to make a career decision.

Those who have already chosen a career in the child care field can enjoy this book as a unique resource for new and exciting career opportunities within the field.

The numerous job opportunities discussed within this book represent hours of research, telephone contacts, day care center visitations, and personal interviews. Although the salaries and job requirements as stated may change, the valuable information gives you a broad picture of the types of jobs available in locations all across America.

You will also note that we have included a special curriculum section. Not only will this section assist new and veteran caregivers, it will also help our parent readers understand the day-to-day activities their children should be enjoying in a quality day care environment.

Whatever direction you choose, we wish you success . . . and we thank you for your positive contribution to our society.

SECTION I
EXPLORING
CHILD CARE
CAREERS

As part of a career exploration book, this section not only provides background information on the evolution of child care, it also includes details on how to prepare for your career and techniques for job-seeking success.

Section I covers many of the traditional child care job opportunities such as preschool teacher, child care instructor, and family day care provider. However, as we move into the 21st century, you will also appreciate the information on new career opportunities. Many of these jobs are still evolving and may be known by other titles or classifications in your state. Once you have explored these careers, you may even discover a hidden niche that only you can fill in the child care field.

Today, more than ever before, child care professionals are becoming pioneers in an industry that will continue to grow for years to come. I hope this information will encourage you to take the first step in seeking a career in the exciting field of child care.

1. Understanding the Child Development Field

Child care, one of today's fastest growing career fields, opens new and exciting doors to those who choose to be involved. Almost 65 percent of mothers with children under age six work outside the home. During the next few years, a record number of mothers, some 50 percent, will be back to work before their infants reach their first birthdays.

With these dramatic changes in the work force, potentially profitable new careers in Early Childhood Education (ECE) are increasing the demand for qualified personnel. Often, twenty times as many jobs are available as there are applicants to fill them.

Twenty years ago people entering the child care field had few career choices. With the opening of Head Start twenty-five years ago, followed by the concept of Child Care Resource & Referral agencies some twelve years ago, the picture for career opportunities in the child care field began changing. Today, career alternatives are being offered in new areas, such as extended day programs, corporate on-site child care programs, and professionally trained nannies. And still the field continues to grow.

Job seekers should consider both the new and the traditional types of child care programs available today before making a final career decision. Following is a partial list of child care career opportunities:

- Child Day Care Centers
- Infant Centers
- Employer-related Centers
- Subsidized Centers
- Nursery Schools
- Extended-day Care Centers (Also called Before and After School Program or Latch Key Center)
- Laboratory Schools
- Religious-oriented Day Care Centers
- Child Care Resource & Referral Agencies
- Family Day Care
- Government Programs
- Child Care Consulting
- Child Care Coordinators

HISTORICAL ROOTS OF EARLY CHILDHOOD EDUCATION

Early childhood education rises out of a long historical tradition. Knowledge about this history and its contributing theorists gives us insight into the philosophies that are incorporated in today's early childhood programs. Standards of measuring normal development in children were developed by many of these theorists, and today they are used by child care professionals who work with children.

Oftentimes, a prospective employer in a large school will ask you questions on this subject. For example, you might be asked: "Do you apply Piaget in your curriculum planning? Do you agree with this philosophy?"

Following are developmental views by theorists who have contributed significantly to setting standards for measuring the development of young children:

Humanistic/Maturational Views

The early theorists who developed humanistic/maturational views were concerned with such issues as the education of the whole child, the interrelationship of the mind and the body, and the role of play in learning. Educators have labeled this the "Maturational Approach" or the "Whole Child Approach."

Humanistic traditions date back to Plato and Aristotle (420 B.C.) Both men recognized the importance of introducing children to education in their early years. Viewing humans as essentially good, they wanted to create a society of good people who followed good laws.

During the Middle Ages, religious reformers and philosophers such as Martin Luther, John Comenius, and Jean Rousseau contributed their ideas of learning through play. Johann H. Pestalozi, an early 1800s Swiss philosopher, believed that education should be based on the natural development of children and every child is capable of learning.

Charles Darwin, in his late 19th century book, *Expression of the Emotions in Man and Animals*, tells about observing his seven children. He brought back to educators the idea that children have natural and understandable emotions. When children cry, there is a reason for the tears. They may have been hurt. (For example, he once unknowingly caused crying by brushing his baby's face with his cufflink.)

Other educators during Darwin's time believed that children were alien dolls, miniaturized adults, or empty slates and sponges, ready to absorb knowledge.

Cognitive Approach

Another perspective in child development is the cognitive approach to learning. Philosophers who hold this view are primarily concerned with the intellectual development of the child.

Jean Piaget, considered the founder of this approach, devoted many years in the early 20th century to the study of a child's thought process. He believed that the process was fundamentally different from that of adults. Children are not adults in miniature form; rather, they have their own distinct ways of determining reality and viewing the world. Piaget believed that a child's mental development progressed through certain stages.

Those who hold this view believe in allowing the child to accumulate meaningful experiences in his or her daily environment, at home and at school. Early childhood professionals who incorporate Piaget's ideas into school curriculum see these objectives as helping children in their thinking processes.

Behaviorist Approach

Another perspective on development, proposed by psychologists, can be labeled as the behaviorist approach. Behaviorist theories argue that the only successful method of learning is based on conclusions derived from observing behavioral changes in children after they have been systematically rewarded for their progress. They believe that the simple conditioning techniques used to shape the behavior of animals can be used with humans. In this view, the child is seen as responding to the environment.

Gesell Approach

Earlier this century, Arnold Gesell became interested in body growth and how it influenced child development in relationship to the environment. His theories were based on behavioral tests designed to measure the maturational levels of children. These tests are still used in measuring children for kindergarten admission.

Psychosocial Development Theory

This viewpoint on child development focuses on inner processes and emotional development. Sigmund Freud is considered the father of this theory. He worked with emotionally troubled parents to conceptualize his therapeutic theory into a framework that was accepted at the turn of this century. Freud believed that the early experiences of a child affected his or her behavior and personality in the adult years.

Eric Erickson, born in 1902 and a disciple of Freud, is noted for his book, *Childhood and Society*. In the book, he describes eight stages of man's emotional development. Basically, he believed that individuals must go through behavior crises to develop healthy, strong emotional lives. Each stage must be completed and the crisis resolved before the child can progress to the next stage.

AGES AND STAGES

Infants and Toddlers

Infants who are placed in a day care setting, even as young as six weeks, thrive and grow just as well as infants who spend time with only one primary caregiver. The methods for getting babies off to a good start come naturally with the baby's help.

All infants try hard to identify their primary caregivers, whether that person is the mother, a day care center teacher, or a family day care provider. This person becomes important in the early nurturing and protection process. As an infant's teacher you have the privilege of helping him or her develop into the wonderful person he or she is meant to be. Following are suggestions for helping the infant develop:

- Follow the baby's feeding and sleeping schedule. Always hold the baby for bottle feeding, preferably at an angle to reduce the risk of an ear infection.
- Create an interesting and safe environment for the baby. Choose toys that are safe and appropriate to the baby's age. Keep in mind that babies do a lot of chewing, grasping, and dropping.
- To develop basic trust, develop an environment that stimulates all five senses.

It doesn't take infants long to develop physical-emotional closeness with their primary caregivers. Those who make a career decision to work with infants will reap the rewards of satisfaction in helping infants develop into loving, caring children and adults.

During the interview process for an ECE position, you may be asked questions about planning curriculum for certain age groups. The following chart will familiarize you with the various ages and stages.

Infant Development (0-12 Months)

0-3 Months: Gaining control of eyes, head, neck and shoulders. Enjoys looking at objects—birds, open windows.

3-6 Months: Developing upper body control. Propped up for short periods. Reaching and grasping. Likes bright colors. Puts things in mouth.

6-9 Months: Sits steadily without support. Pulls up on bar in crib or playpen. May begin creeping on floor. Falls easily.

9-12 Months: Uses playpen to pull up and try legs. Clutches on playpen while attempting walking steps. If the child is not walking by 15 months, a bouncer or walker on wheels often adds security. Once the child is walking, push and pull toys are essential as an incentive to learn about the environment.

Infant's Point of View

0-3 Months: "I'm totally dependent on others to survive. I can't make choices. When I get excited, I kick my feet and wave my arms as fast as I possibly can."

3-6 Months: "Oh, how I love that plastic ring. Don't be surprised, I sometimes act shy or afraid. Bring new people to me one at a time."

6-9 Months: "Give me something to hold. Sometimes something on my gums feels good. Talk to me, I like it."

9-12 Months: "Give me time to look and explore: I am a curious person. I am learning to talk and walk. I get tense when I have to face a new situation such as strangers, animals, loud noises, or the dark. I cry because I can't talk and tell you about all my fears."

Toddler Development (12-27 Months)

9-15 Months: Cooperates in playing pat-a-cake. Walks, holding onto furniture and sturdy objects. Child stands unsupported; doesn't hold onto anything or any person. May be unsteady, but can stand for about a minute. Looks at pictures of him/herself in a baby book.

11-15 Months: Neat pincer grasp, similar to picking up raisins. Indicates or gestures needs and wants without crying. Child uses some sound or motion such as shaking head "no," pointing or holding out arms to tell you he wants to be picked up. Imitates words (record which words are used).

12-18 Months: Turns pages of books. Has a vocabulary of words other than "mommy" and "daddy." Stacks blocks two or three high. Scribbles spontaneously. Uses pencil or crayon and makes marks on any surface.

15-22 Months: Removes simple garments. Child takes off shoes, socks, pants, etc., without help if unfastened. Walks backward. Stacks blocks three or more high. Walks up steps with help. Child walks upright, not on all fours, using wall, handrail, or a person's hand. Two feet on a step at a time is usual.

15-27 Months: Throws ball overhand. Child throws ball without regard to direction or distance. Runs with confidence. Uses spoon, spills. Ask child, "What is this?" Can name three pictures in a book. Uses words to make wants known. Uses real words or play words. For example, "milk," "go potty," "want cracker," "bye-bye."

Preschool Development (2-5 Years)

The preschool child, ages two to five, is in a continuous process of growth and change. The normal child goes through several child development stages. By studying these growth stages, you'll know what to expect.

18 ■ CAREERS IN CHILD CARE

The way you react to children's needs influences how they grow. An awareness of how and what children learn at these various stages will help you plan activities to encourage the children's growth. Remember, it's more important for a child to feel respected and wanted than it is for him to count or know his alphabet at a certain stage of growth. Children learn more easily and more quickly when they have a sense of self-worth.

Preschool children, just like infants, learn by using their five senses. Their ideas and concepts are formed by action experiences (Piaget) such as tasting, touching, and feeling. As the child grows older, he learns through language.

WORD PICTURES OF DEVELOPMENT

Two Year Old

Affective
Self-centered, "me" and "mine"
Can't share
Watches others
Complete dependence on adults

Cognitive
Investigative — touch, taste
Can't recognize problems
One or two words with objects
Wide vocabulary range of 5-1,200 words

Motor
Whole-body action
Walks up and down stairs alone
Hand preference development
Dependent on adults for dressing

Three Year Old

Affective
Highly imitative of adults
Enjoys contacts with people, especially adults
Wants to please adults
Goes after what he wants, fights for it

Cognitive
Makes simple choices
Lively imagination
Moves and talks at the same time
Talks about non-present situations

Motor
Well-balanced body lines
Can carry liquids
Rides a tricycle
Puts on, takes off wraps with some help

Four Year Old

Affective
Dominates, bossy, boastful
Hits, grabs for what he wants
Cooperative play with two or three others
Resistant, tests limits

Cognitive
Discovers forms while using materials
Attention span: 8-12 minutes
Uses "bathroom words," swears
Able to talk to solve conflicts

Motor
A long, leaner body
Can jump about own height and land upright
Throws large ball, kicks with some accuracy
Can't set limits—active until exhausted

Five Year Old

Affective
Becoming poised, self-confident
Aware of rules, defines them for others
Conscious of sex difference of playmates, sex play
Talks about home, possessions, reveals family secrets

Cognitive
Curious about everything
Knows name and address
Likes to be busy making "something," industrious
Assertive in use of language—"I already know that."

Motor
Enjoys activities requiring hand skills
Draws a recognizable man
Enjoys jumping, running, stunting
Surging physical drives

Six to Eight Year Old

Affective
Beginning to turn interest to other adults, such as Scout leaders and teachers
Shares ideas and interests with friends
Enjoys team games and board games such as checkers

Cognitive
Entering stage of concrete operations, such as adding and subtracting
Beginning to read
Enjoys making presents for family and friends

Motor
Likes to try new adventures
Can learn to ride bicycle without training wheels
Aggressive with body, using large muscles
Seven year olds like pencils, paper, coloring, using small muscles

Eight to Ten Year Old

Affective
Becomes more disillusioned with the shortcomings of parents and adults
Relies on companions for support and cooperation
Team play is popular; likes to decide the rules

Cognitive
Likes to initiate new activities
Capable of abstract thought and can think about things
Takes things seriously
Greater memory capacity; can explain an enjoyable book or TV show

Motor
Stands and balances with ease
Takes pride in physical appearance
Likes to take care of himself or herself

IMPORTANCE OF PLAY IN PRESCHOOL DEVELOPMENT

Information on the importance of play is necessary for prospective child care workers. ECE interviewees are frequently asked about the value of play in a child's learning process. Children learn from play in a way nothing else can teach. After watching children, we can understand the saying that play is "a child's work."

Many theories about play have been studied. Over a hundred years ago, German-born Frederick Frobel started what is known today as a kindergarten program and gave direction for using play to help children grow.

The "recreation" theory maintains that tension can be released and relaxation takes over through play. The "preparatory" theory considers play to be the primary preparation for future life and work. When children create make-believe play, they are preparing for their future roles in society. Educators consider play to have value, giving youngsters the potential for learning about themselves and the world.

Observers in most ECE programs see how children's natural activities, such as block play, playing house, and other creative activities, have value in educational programs. Symbolic toys for fantasy play and toys for using small and large muscles also serve as legitimate educational activities for play learning.

As a prospective employee in a day care center, you might be asked about play. For instance, you might be asked to give an example of how children learn through block play. Here is an appropriate response:

"Playing with blocks can be beneficial in several ways. As a child builds houses, roads, towers, etc., he learns to hold onto an idea and carry out his building plan. This develops his thinking skills. For example, if the child puts one or two blocks together to push along, the blocks symbolize a real object such as a train. When he sees or rides on a train, he then masters the real meaning of the word 'train'. By understanding the concept of trains and making the blocks into an object, he is beginning to learn the process of reading.

"Based on a symbol system, reading requires an understanding of the written word. For example, you have to experience a real birthday party to understand what 'birthday party' means."

2. Goal Setting and Training Programs

EVALUATING YOUR PERSONAL NEEDS

Making a lifetime career choice isn't always easy. You will have to come to terms with your goals and personal characteristics before deciding on the type of training you will need to work with young children and their families. Before making a career decision in the Early Childhood Education (ECE) field, ask yourself if you are suitable for this type of career. Your decision is a little like baking a cake. You need the instructions, right ingredients, and the correct temperature to make the cake taste good. Following are the main ingredients for working with children:

1. Knowledge of current child care practices and the ability to disseminate this information to both children and parents.
2. A nurturing disposition, one that shows empathy, warmth, and caring for children and families.
3. Understanding and respecting young children's needs.
4. Ability to plan and create a good learning environment.
   Just as the temperature is important when baking a cake, the "temperament," or nature, of the caregiver is important too.
5. Understanding yourself and how you view the world and make decisions.
6. Good physical and mental health.
7. Sensitivity to others, yet a positive attitude about your own sense of self-worth.

In order to work with children you must understand children. They are unique human beings; no two are alike. Each child develops at his or her own pace. Growth and development are affected by such variables as genetics and environment. Inherited characteristics influence such things as body build and mental abilities. Environmental differences create different personalities. Therefore, no two children can be handled in exactly the same way. The "Ages and Stages" chart found in Chapter 1 will help you select the age group with which you prefer to work.

SETTING GOALS

In today's child care marketplace, careers are changing daily to meet the needs of parents, children, businesses, public schools, and local communities. As you explore this book, you'll begin to see the wide scope of career options available today. To find out where you fit in, take a few minutes and ask yourself these six questions:

- Am I interested in educating and caring for children?
- What area of the child care field interests me?
- Do I enjoy working with children of all ages? Or would I prefer to work with one specific age group — infants, toddlers, preschool children, or school-age children?
- Am I interested in serving families?
- Am I interested in working with the public sector of child care? Or would I prefer working in a corporate or business-related child care program?
- Am I interested in child care issues?

If you discover that you are particularly interested in working directly with young children, take a few minutes and answer the questions on this self-evaluation quiz:

MAKING THE RIGHT DECISION

Self-Evaluation for the Early Childhood Teacher

I am like this:	This is something I can learn:	When people say, "This is an effective teacher," they mean that she/he:

Personal Qualities and Classroom Presence

❏	❏	Acts relaxed and comfortable, yet alert
❏	❏	Maintains good eye contact, often getting down to the child's eye level
❏	❏	Speaks with a voice that is gentle, quiet, calm, and firm, sending messages that are direct and clear
❏	❏	Has a special voice for talking to children
❏	❏	Has a clean, healthy, professional appearance and wears clothes appropriate to the day's work
❏	❏	Listens carefully and respectfully
❏	❏	Has a high tolerance for variety of noise and movement and doesn't expect order every moment
❏	❏	Touches children often with movements that soothe, guide, redirect, reassure, reinforce

Teaching Style and Strategies

❏	❏	Enjoys children and expresses genuine interest in them
❏	❏	Is willing to learn from children and follow their lead
❏	❏	Is able to focus on individual children while being aware of

☐ ☐ what is happening throughout the classroom
☐ ☐ Relates to each child's personality and developmental level
☐ ☐ Uses positive statements
☐ ☐ Is empathetic — able to feed back to the child an understanding of feelings behind his words or behavior
☐ ☐ Makes opportunities for one-to-one activities with children
☐ ☐ Is aware of differing moods of children, adjusts standards for them when they are fatigued, irritated, overstimulated, stressed
☐ ☐ Remains in control in startling or difficult situations
☐ ☐ Enjoys humorous incidents with children; enjoys laughing with them
☐ ☐ Actively participates with children, has a plan for each day—goals to be accomplished
☐ ☐ Sets consistent, realistic limits and focuses on the behaviors (not the child)
☐ ☐ Provides guidance in development of good habits for eating, resting, toileting, learning, exercise
☐ ☐ Responsive to the rhythms and tempos of the child
☐ ☐ Shows enthusiasm for the day, coming up with new and interesting ideas and activities to share with children
☐ ☐ Supports cultural differences
☐ ☐ Positions self naturally in strategic spots

Environment/Climate Design

☐ ☐ Creates an environment where children are comfortable enough to verbalize their feelings
☐ ☐ Creates an atmosphere that is comfortable, home-like, safe
☐ ☐ Provides an organized structured schedule to reassure children
☐ ☐ Fosters inquisitiveness about physical world
☐ ☐ Facilitates social interactions among children
☐ ☐ Questions and explores with children so that all learn through discovery
☐ ☐ Maintains an organized, clean classroom
☐ ☐ Tends to repairs
☐ ☐ Considers the outdoors part of the learning environment

Relationship to Other Teachers

☐ ☐ Accepts criticism and is responsive to changes
☐ ☐ Gets along well with others
☐ ☐ Asks for help when needed
☐ ☐ Is quick to express approval and support for other staff
☐ ☐ Is willing to listen to suggestions and other ideas but not just a "yes" person
☐ ☐ Is aware of other teachers' needs in classroom and prepared to take over when necessary
☐ ☐ Is slow about making judgments and sensitive in sharing negative feedback
☐ ☐ Risks sharing of self and abilities, ideas and strengths
☐ ☐ Is a team player, provides ongoing training to new teachers, involves other staff in planning

Relationship to Parents

☐ ☐ Communicates with parents at drop-off and pick-up times, and as needed throughout the day
☐ ☐ Schedules parent conferences when needed
☐ ☐ Does not discuss a child's behavior when he is present
☐ ☐ Respects families' right to privacy by not discussing problems with others
☐ ☐ Assists parents with goals for children
☐ ☐ Perceives self as part of a support system to parents, someone whose role is to strengthen the family unit
☐ ☐ Is able to make parents aware of their strengths
☐ ☐ Uses the insights of parents about their children
☐ ☐ Is available to parents

Professional Responsibilities

☐ ☐ Attends regular staff meetings and workshops
☐ ☐ Attends to all four areas of human development in planning —affective, social, psychomotor, and cognitive
☐ ☐ Conscientious effort to expand knowledge of good early childhood teaching
☐ ☐ Willing to try something new — not afraid to risk failing/mistakes
☐ ☐ Manages time well
☐ ☐ Demonstrates pride in being a child care teacher
☐ ☐ Takes advantage of opportunities provided

This form was developed and published (April 1989) by *Child Care Information Exchange*, a bimonthly management publication for owners and directors, P.O. Box 2890, Redmond, WA 98052.

VALUES — PREPARING FOR YOUR CAREER

Values are those things we perceive as desirable. They are qualities prized for themselves, such as love, wisdom, beauty, and knowing right from wrong. Some of the values agreed upon by ECE professionals for children in day care settings include: children are to be respected for their individuality and those differences that make them unique; day care workers should help children develop social, emotional, physical, and intellectual skills; as a caregiver, your primary responsibility will be to care for the children throughout the day.

To enrich your ECE values you might want to volunteer to work in a day care center. There you can interact with the children in a variety of ways. Children enjoy stories, play, and other creative activities. Consider taking an ECE college course such as child development, multicultural curriculum, family and community relations, or psychology.

SUCCESSFUL PEOPLE . . .

Successful people, whether in the child care field or other careers, have several important traits. How do you measure up as a successful person?

Successful people . . .

. . . see their entire life as their "career"—not just their work.
. . . know the difference between the important and the trivial.
. . . don't get sidetracked by other people's agendas. They follow their own.
. . . are well aware of their flaws and their talents and do not chastise themselves for their weaknesses. They stress the positive.
. . . see mistakes as challenges to learn from rather than as failures. At the same time, they know when to cut their losses.
. . . value their time. They only spread themselves thin if they think it will pay off. They do not necessarily equate being "busy" with being successful.
. . . are not motivated by the need for security alone.
. . . spend more energy problem-solving than on drawbacks to projects.
. . . know the power of inner discipline.
. . . learn from others.

TEACHER'S TRAINING PROGRAMS

In order to achieve your particular career goals in the field of child care, you will likely need some type of training. In years past, people were hired in this field simply because they had an interest in children or could work well with children and/or the staff. However, during the past decade, most states have enacted legislation requiring child care staff to have formal training to prepare them for their work with children. Even if your state has not enacted legislation, hiring personnel will be looking for the best qualified person, one who has had child development training.

Nothing will show your commitment to your career as well as your willingness to learn and your desire to educate yourself in caring for children. By taking classes, you show that you are not only enriching your knowledge, but that you have your eye on the future.

College Course Work/Two-Year Associate Training

The child development programs offered at community colleges provide the competency that child caregivers need for employment as teachers, teacher assistants, and directors in all types of centers—private day care, preschools, and publicly funded programs.

Courses in community colleges are designed to help students become familiar with the basic issues in child development, curriculum development, the parenting process, and the impact of the family, the community, and the school on the growing child.

In states such as California and Illinois, at least twelve units of college course work are required for employment in the child development field. In order to have greater choices in job opportunities, today's child caregiver should attain his or her two-year associate degree.

Sample Course Work in Two-Year Training Program
- Introduction to Careers with Children
- Child Study and Observation
- Child Growth and Development
- Principles and Practices in Early Childhood Programs
- Creative Science and Math for Young Children
- Health and Safety of Young Children
- Infant/Toddler Care

Associated Arts Degree in Early Childhood Education

For an Associated Arts (AA) degree in Early Childhood Education, you will need to meet the college's general education requirements along with your child development courses. At most community colleges, sixty semester units will be required for this degree. Some of the general requirements include humanities, social sciences, math, science, English, speech, history, psychology, and sociology.

This degree gives you a solid educational background and prepares you to work with children, families, and community programs. One advantage of the AA degree is that it may be transferable to a four-year university should you decide to continue your education and obtain a Bachelor's degree.

Numerous child care career opportunities are available to those who have AA or Bachelor's degrees.

Child Development Associate Program

The Child Development Associate (CDA) Program was implemented in 1973 as a credentials program that provides in-service training, assessment, and credentials experiences.

As defined by the Child Development Associate Consortium, a child development associate is an early childhood professional who assumes primary responsibility for meeting the specific needs of a group of children in a child development setting by nurturing the children physically, socially, emotionally, and intellectually. As a child care professional, you will set up and maintain the child care environment and establish a relationship between parents and the center. Phases of the CDA program include field work, instructional course work, and orientation and evaluation.

The CDA credential is awarded to those who successfully complete the CDA assessment process. Many states have incorporated these credentials into their child care licensing requirements. Since awarding the first credential in 1975, more than 30,000 individuals have received the CDA credential.

CDA Competency Goals
- To establish and maintain a safe, healthy learning environment.
- To advance physical and intellectual competency.
- To support social and emotional development and provide guidance.
- To establish positive and productive relationships with families.
- To ensure a well-run, purposeful program that is responsive to the participants' needs.
- To maintain a commitment to professionalism.

The CDA assessment is accomplished through an evaluation by the CDA national credential program. The evaluation team is made up of the participant, an early childhood professional, a member of the community, and a CDA representative. Each of the team members observes and collects information about the candidate's work in relation to the competency standards.

The candidate must work with an advisor for at least twelve weeks. Since candidates work at their own pace, many finish in a few months, while others take one or two years.

In September 1990, the CDA Council instituted a new professional training model. The purpose is to develop nationally a strong core of child care workers. This one-year program will qualify individuals for an early childhood profession. To enroll, you will be required to submit an application along with a fee.

More information about the CDA credential may be obtained by calling or writing:

COUNCIL FOR EARLY CHILDHOOD PROFESSIONAL RECOGNITION
1718 Connecticut Ave. NW, Suite 500
Washington, DC 20009
(202) 265-9090 or (800) 424-4310

High/Scope® Educational Research Foundation

High/Scope® Educational Research Foundation is a non-profit organization that has done extensive research on teaching styles, classroom curriculum models, and child development. This research has resulted in a program that addresses the developmental needs of preschoolers, and is called "cognitively oriented" curriculum.

High/Scope® offers many on-site teacher training programs throughout the United States, including a two-day workshop, which is co-sponsored with a local agency.

The main components of the High/Scope® program are:

A consistent daily routine with a time set aside for each child to plan for an activity, work at the activity, and tell about the activity when he or she is finished. High/Scope calls this the "Plan, Do, Review." This process helps foster independence and responsibility in children, helps them focus on what they're doing, and promotes language skills. Other parts of the daily routine include small group time, large group time, and outdoor time.

Arrangement of room and materials so children know what may be done and where the materials may be found. The room is divided into at least four work areas—house, art, block, and quiet. The shelves and materials in the room are labeled so children can get them out and put them away by themselves.

Key experiences are presented so children will become actively involved in what they're doing. These key experiences form the content of the curriculum.

Team teaching, with all classroom staff and volunteers working together, forms the basis of the teaching plan and its implementation in the classroom.

Staff training gives the program a solid foundation.

The rationale and implementation of the cognitively oriented curriculum is a course in itself developed by High/Scope®. It is called the "Training of Trainers" program. High/Scope® trains teachers in how to set up classrooms and how to train other teachers in their centers. The training of trainers consists of seven sessions, each one week long.

For more information about this program, write or call:

HIGH/SCOPE® EDUCATION RESEARCH FOUNDATION
600 N. River St.
Ypsilanti, MI 48198
(313) 485-2000

3. Techniques for Job-Seeking Success

FINDING THE RIGHT JOB

As a prospective child care employee, you might view résumés, job interviews, and cover letters as hurdles to leap over in obtaining the job you desire. In actuality, résumés, cover letters, and interviews can work for you. They are not methods of keeping you from a job. They simply show an employer what you know and what you can do.

One way to meet prospective child care employers is to increase your visibility at the right places. Attend meetings, workshops, and seminars relating to child care issues. To find out about these events in your community, call the local Child Care Resource & Referral agency or the national or local affiliates of the National Association for the Education of Young Children (NAEYC).

Costs for most of the conferences and workshops are quite reasonable. For example, one recent Southern California Association for the Education of Young Children workshop cost $15 and attracted more than 1,400 attendees. The conference offered thirty-six different workshops, all dealing with child care issues. Get your feet wet at one of these conferences and learn about children, families, child care policies, and legislation that affects child care workers.

Once you've made up your mind to get a job in the child care field, it's just a question of which one suits you. Teacher shortages are at an all-time high, and applying for a job at a day care center isn't complicated. They usually have short applications form and quick interviews.

Let's take a closer look at the procedures that may be required when applying for a child care position. Many employers will require applications, résumés, cover letters, and interviews.

RECIPE FOR A SUPER RÉSUMÉ

Résumés give the employer written evidence of your qualifications in better form than an application. Basically, there are two types of résumés: chronological and functional. The type of résumé you select depends on your experience.

Gathering the Ingredients

Before putting your résumé together, you'll need to assess your abilities, skills, interests, education, and work experience. The task of gathering information is neither easy nor quick. However, it may be the most important step in writing your résumé. The average employer skims a résumé in one minute; therefore, it must be clear and concise.

There are no perfect or right résumé formats. Although the chronological form is the most common, the functional form can also be effective. When writing the functional form, rank everything in order of importance, starting with the most important and ending with the least important. Since résumés are read from left to right, those items that enter the memory first are usually the ones remembered.

Basic Ingredients

Name, current address, telephone number: If you are rarely home during business hours, list the phone number of a friend or relative who will take messages for you.

Career objective: Include a brief statement if you have a specific career objective—type of work or position desired. Following are some examples:

To obtain a position in an Early Childhood Education program.

To join a day care program that offers an opportunity to utilize the experience and creativity of an energetic and responsible individual.

To obtain a management position in an educational environment requiring strong administrative and supervisory skills.

To become a director of a multi-disciplinary child development program.

To obtain a position enabling me to use my interpersonal and organizational skills in an Early Childhood Education program.

Education: List the highest level of formal education first, your major or minor, and your date of graduation or the anticipated date of graduation. If you have attended Early Childhood Education (ECE) workshops and seminars or had in-service training at your last job, list these. Following are some examples:

- June 1989—Mt. San Antonio Community College, Walnut, CA, Nursery School Certificate, Associated Arts degree, expected completion June 1990.
- September 1986-Present—Attended and participated in various seminars and conferences emphasizing child development and teaching skills. (National Association for the Education of Young Children, Southern California Association for the Education of Young Children, American Christian Schools International)

Experience: Your experience includes both paid and volunteer positions. In the child care field, all volunteer work, whether at church or for an organization, may be listed on your résumé. Prospective employers are looking for applicants who can handle and plan activities for groups of children of varying ages.

To describe your work experience, first analyze your jobs. Use descriptive titles and list your duties. Following are some examples:

HEAD TODDLER TEACHER
South East YWCA Daycare
Denver, CO
(Responsibilities for children 18 months to 3 years included planning and implementing morning curriculum such as circle time, small groups, free play, art and gym activities. Other responsibilities included classroom management, directing assistant teacher, and planning field trips.)

DIRECTOR
Agency for Child Development
Brooklyn, NY
(Administered large child care program, which served over 200 families and was composed of both infant/toddlers and school-age children. Major responsibilities included coordinating a staff of 20 people, scheduling, curriculum and program development, budget compliance, and accounts receivable. Public relations specialties included promoting agency events at community programs, conferences, and social programs for staff and parents.)

DIRECTOR
New Christian Church
New Orleans, LA
(Responsibilities included recruitment and enrollment of 60 children, staff hiring, budget compliance, curriculum planning, purchasing materials and supplies, and practicing Christian principles.)

SELECTING A RÉSUMÉ FORMAT

Now that you've gathered the basic ingredients, let's take a look how to put it all together. See examples on pages 32 and 33.

Finding the Right Words

We all have personality strengths and weaknesses. There are no rights or wrongs in mentioning personal assets on your résumé or during the interview process. When considering applicants for an ECE position, employers want to match the right person to the job. The personal assets you list in your résumé will help employers make this match.

Functional Format

This type of format stresses what you can do. The information is arranged in the order of importance rather than by a time sequence. The functional format allows you to highlight major areas of accomplishments, strengths, and abilities.

Cynthia Quinn
1111 Terrace Drive
Covina, CA 99999
(444) 000-8900

OBJECTIVE: To obtain a position in an Early Childhood Education program.

QUALIFICATIONS: Successfully developed and implemented an extended day care program for 1st - 6th grade students. Developed functional forms and procedures to maintain attendance, bookkeeping and budget records.

Successfully planned and conducted daily activities for preschool class. Responsibilities included writing children's assessments and communicating daily with the parents.

Worked in a team developing, planning, and implementing curriculum, and supervising small and large groups of children as a student teacher.

EDUCATION: AA Degree - 1982
Mt. San Antonio Community College
Walnut, CA
(12 semester units in Early Childhood Education)
Attended various seminars and conferences sponsored by the National Association for the Education of Young Children.

Chronological Format

This type of format arranges information in a time sequence.

Bette White
1234 20th Street
Pittsfield, MA 22222
(222) 000-0000

CAREER OBJECTIVE: To establish myself as an effective teacher of young children in a multi-ethnic setting.

WORK EXPERIENCE:

<u>Teacher</u>
Church of the Saints 1988 - Present
Pittsfield, MA
(Duties include planning daily activities which include specific objectives to meet the social/emotional, physical and intellectual needs of a three-year-old class.)

A.B.C. Nursery School 1985-1988
Albany, NY
(Duties included planning, implementing, supervising and evaluating lessons and activities for a four-year-old class.)

<u>Sunday School Teacher</u>
Methodist Church 1983-1985
Albany, NY
(Volunteer position at church each Sunday. Responsible for a group of 15 children, teaching Bible stories and planned art activities.)

EDUCATION:
Albany Community College 1983-1985
Albany, NY
(15 semester units in Early Childhood Education)
Primary goal is to obtain an Associate of Arts degree in Early Childhood Education.

REFERENCES AVAILABLE UPON REQUEST

✓

In a recent survey of top managers, 50 percent rated "the ability to get along with people" as the most important asset. Here are some adjective choices for you to consider as you describe your strengths.

aware	caring
humorous	responsible
open	practical
active	creative
calm	sensitive
energetic	even-tempered
capable	adaptable
supportive	

IMPORTANCE OF A COVER LETTER

A cover letter serves several important purposes: it introduces your résumé, explains how your background matches the position, and asks for an interview. Always use a cover letter when you're mailing your résumé. The first paragraph of your cover letter should explain why you are qualified for the job, the second paragraph should refer to accomplishments on the résumé, and the third paragraph should ask for the interview and mention the best time to reach you.

Sample Cover Letter

```
Dear Ms. Smith:

    I feel that my education and experience in child care would
be an asset to your day care program. I would welcome the
opportunity of working with you and your staff.
    As you will note on my enclosed resume, I am capable of
working with children of all ages. I also enjoy writing student
assessments and working with the parents.
    I am available every day after 3:00 p.m. Could we schedule
a personal interview to discuss my background in greater
detail?

Sincerely,

Jane Doe
```

HANDLING THE INTERVIEW

Teaching Position

You can study and read all types of material to determine whether you're the right person for the job, but basically it boils down to three important questions the interviewing team will want answered: Do you have enough knowledge of child development to put it to practical use in the classroom? Do you have behavior management skills? For example, do you know how to handle children's fights or children who disrupt the classroom? And, how do you handle angry parents?

With this information in mind, think about the day-to-day operation of a day care center, and know what your role as a teacher will be before you go into the interview.

10 Questions Most Commonly Asked of Teacher Applicants

1. Why do you want to work with young children?
2. What do you like or dislike about your present job position? Your past job position?
3. What are some good books to read to three year olds?
4. What daily activities would you plan for four year olds?
5. How would you handle children who are fighting over a toy?
6. How do you handle a toddler who bites?
7. If you could design your own classroom what materials would you choose?
8. How do you feel about working in a multi-ethnic setting?
9. How do you handle an angry parent?
10. This job may involve lifting, diapering, and toileting. Do you have any objections? Is there any reason you may not be able to perform these duties?

Management Position

As with teaching positions, the interviewing team will be looking for the right match. They will be taking a close look at your capabilities — good judgment, written and oral communication skills, and fiscal management skills. Keep in mind the phrase, "the buck stops here." You'll have to convey the image that you're fully capable of being in charge of the entire operation.

For management positions you are usually asked, either on the application or during the interview, to include a sample paragraph describing your philosophy of child care, child development, and/or a statement of your objectives and goals in education.

Following are some sample philosophical points you can use when seeking employment. More than likely you can be just as creative in developing your own statements.

"As director of a day care center, I plan to provide a healthy, happy environment where children have the opportunity to explore and create with materials provided at the center. I believe children should be able to choose materials and activities in a relaxed atmosphere. Children are our natural resources and should be nurtured. Each and every child should be respected for his own unique qualities."

"My philosophy of child care and development is both experiential and theoretical. The three theoretical models on which I base my philosophy are Piaget's cognitive concepts, Gesell's age/stage theory, and Erickson's study of personality growth."

"I view the child development field as an integral part of the educational system. My general goal is to consider children, parents, teachers, and the community as the centers of the day care system."

10 Questions Most Commonly Asked of Management Applicants

1. How do you coordinate the following day care center functions? Staff recruitment; staff training; firing a staff member; scheduling employee hours; and facility maintenance.
2. What are some of the health and safety regulations as they relate to child care?
3. What are some of the state and federal regulations as they relate to child care?
4. How do you develop, implement, and evaluate programs to meet the educational, social, and physical needs of children ranging from infants to pre-teens?
5. How would you go about developing a public relations program to recruit children to the center?
6. Do you have methods for forming a liaison with parents?
7. What are some of the fiscal responsibilities in running a child care center?
8. What are your methods of purchasing materials, equipment, supplies, and food?
9. What type of records do you keep?
10. Why is it important to work with other community agencies?

4. Private Sector Careers

A CLOSER LOOK AT TODAY'S JOB OPPORTUNITIES

Child care issues are hot topics for the 1990s. Parents, policy makers, and business leaders are now concerned about the quality, affordability, and availability of child care. Although these concerned citizens want to be involved with child care issues, they tend to leave out the most important person—the child care worker, the person who works directly with youngsters. And they forget the most important issue—compensation. This chapter is devoted to these energetic, caring, responsible people who work with youngsters and their families on a daily basis.

The high demand for child care services has made an impact on the demand for early childhood programs. In many families all the adults are employed. In 1988, 51 percent of the children under age six had mothers in the work force. By 1995, predictions indicate that 15 million children will be in need of some type of child care.

Although the ECE field is striving to attract high-caliber people to this profession, a staffing crisis now exists. Why? Low salaries is the answer. However, this decade shows great promise in arriving at new solutions that will address the issues of poorly paid staff and the high cost of day care rates for parents.

Currently, some 70,000 private day care centers in the United States provide employment for approximately 579,000 ECE workers. Unfortunately, each state has its own titles for day care workers, making it difficult to maintain an accurate census of these workers.

People who work with children in day care centers or preschools, either public or private, are generally called "preschool teachers." Directors or educational coordinators of both part-time and full-time public or private sector programs are usually titled "Early Childhood Administrators." If you care for a child in his or her home, the Bureau of Labor Statistics considers you a "child care worker."

Hopefully, the 1990 census will clarify the titles, thereby giving child care personnel a professional status within the communities at large. The National Association for the Education of Young Children (NAEYC) states: "Accurate data will be especially important to inform public policy makers and planners as decisions concerning early childhood professionals are made in this decade and into the next century."

Another consideration for people looking into employment in the private sector is the child-staff ratio. The maximum number of children permitted per classroom staff is called the child-staff ratio. For example, it could be stated 12:1, meaning twelve children for every staff member. Experts agree that a low child-staff ratio has positive effects on child behavior and staff performance. Each state has different ratios, so it's important for prospective child care workers to know what the child-staff ratio is before applying for a job.

Several trends—the national economy, government priorities for children and their families, and employee fringe benefits—are all playing a role in making child care a national issue and thereby opening new doors of opportunity for the child care professional. With the teacher shortage at an all-time high, your chances for immediate hiring are greatly increased!

WHO'S WHO IN THE PRIVATE SECTOR

Early Childhood Administrator

"I'm the Master of Ceremonies in a three-ring circus," says Judy Thompson, a day care center director. Judy is right; she truly is the most important person in the daily operation of her day care facility. Being able to work with parents, non-professional staff, professional staff, and children is an essential qualification for this position. Good human relations skills are important.

Let's examine the myriad of duties and responsibilities required of a director:

- Responsibility to the governing board of the school, including the establishment of a program philosophy to meet the center's goals.
- Selecting staff, defining staff responsibilities, and supervising all staff.
- Conducting staff meetings to implement school policies and to plan curriculum.
- Maintaining a safe and healthy facility to meet all state regulations.
- Managing all school finances, including collecting fees, budgeting, projecting future expenses, purchasing toys and equipment.
- Ensuring that school curriculum is age-appropriate and meets the physical, intellectual, social, and emotional needs of the children.

According to the 1986 National State of Child Care Regulations, most states are beginning to require administrator's training for directors along with child development course work. The six states that require administrative course work are California, Colorado, Texas, Pennsylvania, Wisconsin, and Virginia.

California, for example, requires candidates for a director's position to have completed a minimum of sixteen units of ECE with three units in Nursery School Administration.

Early Childhood Teachers

The word "teacher" has a variety of meanings. Beyond the literal definitions are the real meanings that come from the hearts and minds of the special people who dedicate themselves to the education and growth of young children.

Young children are growing and learning at a rapid rate. Teachers who guide these youngsters are responsible for providing rich experiences to enhance their growth.

Generally speaking, the person in each classroom who has primary responsibility for the children is considered the teacher. Due to the lack of standard terminology, many programs classify teachers into two categories: teacher and lead (head) teacher. Some states haven't defined the distinctions, leaving the staffing decisions to the director. Usually the head teacher is the trainer of other teachers, a curriculum developer, and a role model for the rest of the staff.

Teachers may also be classified by the age group they oversee. As a job applicant, make sure you're aware of these varying terminologies as well as the responsibilities for each age group.

According to the 1986 National State of Child Care Regulations, eighteen states require training or education for their teachers, seven states have neither educational qualifications nor ongoing training requirements for classroom staff, and thirty-four states have incorporated the Child Development Associate (CDA) into their regulations as one way of qualifying staff in the various roles in licensed programs.

Three states require substantial college course work: California, Illinois, and New Hampshire. Some of the states that don't require training or experience are Arkansas, Kentucky, New Mexico, Utah, Florida, and South Carolina.

CHILD CARE POSITIONS IN THE PRIVATE SECTOR

Infant-Toddler Teacher

This teacher works with infants as young as four weeks old to 2½ years of age. For this age group, some states, such as California, have a

4:1 child-staff ratio.

Duties for the infant-toddler teacher include feeding, changing diapers, and charting information so parents will know how their infants are developing.

Creating an environment that enriches the infant's experiences is most important to his or her development. Caregiver interaction is vitally important to the infant's growth.

Preschool Teacher

Historically the title "preschool teacher" dates back to the 1950s (then sometimes called nursery school teacher"), when child care programs were designed for children ages three to five. These programs were usually morning programs lasting two to three hours. Although many still exist, these programs are dwindling in number as more and more working mothers need ten- to twelve-hour programs. Generally speaking, however, those who work with children ages two through five are still called preschool teachers.

According to the 1986 National State of Child Care Regulation, California mandates a 12:1 child-staff ratio; twelve states have set ratios higher than 12:1, nine states at 15:1; and Texas, North Carolina, and Utah at 25:1 for this age group of children.

The preschool teacher generally has these duties:

- Supervising the physical, emotional, intellectual, and social needs of each child.
- Creating a pleasant, safe environment where each child feels comfortable and secure.
- Maintaining written records for evaluating each child as well as the class as a whole.
- Complying with child care licensing standards, paying particular attention that standards prohibiting corporal punishment are met.

Extended Day Care Teacher (Latchkey Teacher)

These teachers work mainly with children ages five to thirteen and usually in a six-hour position. Most teachers work split shifts or part-time hours. For example, you might work from 6:30 to 8:30 a.m., then return to work from 2:00 to 6:00 p.m.

The child-staff ratio for this position varies from state to state. The ratio in New York is 10:1, while in Florida a state regulatory agency has set the ratio at 25:1.

Duties for extended day care teachers may include providing care, supervision, and individual and recreational activities for a specific age group; administering basic first aid; working with both individual students and/or groups of school-age children; and walking children to and from public school sites.

Teacher Aide/Teacher Assistant

"I'm the chief cook and bottle washer," says Velva Hernandez, who serves as an aide for a child care center in California. An aide's position is extremely vital to the daily operation of a day care center. Aides must have among their skills the ability to relate to young children.

Essentially, the aide works with the teacher, helping enrich the classroom and making the schedule run smoothly and efficiently. Fairness and patience are two necessary personal traits needed in an aide. As a team member of the child care staff, the aide is responsible for meeting the goals of the teacher and the director.

In most states, aide jobs are readily available to high school graduates. No educational requirements are usually necessary for this position. Although it may be an entry level position, the knowledge and experience gained will potentially afford you upward mobility, particularly if you continue your ECE education.

More than half of the aides work less than full-time and generally at an entry level position. The salary is at the minimum wage level. Salaries within local school districts are higher, usually around $6.00 per hour. One irony in the child care field is that an aide working for a school district can earn more than a child care teacher in the private sector.

TYPES OF PROGRAMS

The greatest demand for jobs in the child care field is in the private sector. Generally speaking, private sector jobs are in day care centers, private preschools, and Montessori schools. These programs are supported by parental fees rather than subsidized by government funds. Some preschools are classified as for-profit centers; others are not-for-profit centers such as religious-oriented and parent participation centers.

The Trendwatcher Panel (1989) provides statistics showing that among private sector centers the for-profit centers have expanded more than 20 percent in the past decade.

National Chains

National chains are child care organizations that operate more than 100 centers across the USA. They usually operate on a twelve-hour plus work day, Monday through Friday. The two largest national chains are KinderCare and La Petite.

KinderCare is the largest of the national chains with more than 1,240 centers and 17,000 child care workers. La Petite has more than 750 centers and employs approximately 10,000 workers.

These centers are located mainly in Alabama, Texas, and California. KinderCare has approximately seventy-five centers in California and 138 in Texas, while La Petite boasts of forty centers in Texas.

Regional Chains

Regional chains operate anywhere from two to 100 centers. Gerber's and Children's World fall into this category. Most regional chains are located in California.

Independent Centers

Independent organizations with a single center are classified as non-profit or for-profit agencies. These centers account for nearly 80 percent of all the day care centers. Forrest Day School in Montclair, California is a typical example of a family-operated private proprietary center, which has operated for more than thirty-five years in the same location. Their license capacity is forty-five children.

Employer-Related Child Care Centers

Because child care is projected to be the employee fringe benefit of the 1990s, many large corporations are taking a closer look at on-site child care centers. At present, a broad variety of employer-related programs is available. *Employer-Supported Child Care and Directory of Corporate Child Care* by Dr. Sandra Burud lists more than 3,000 employer-assisted programs.

Many hospitals, such as Methodist Hospital of Southern California, had enough visionary sense to assist their nursing staffs with child care needs back in the 1950s, by opening on-site child care centers. Governmental agencies such as the Department of Motor Vehicles in California and the Department of Transportation in the District of Columbia have now opened on-site day care centers for the children of their employees.

Zale Jewelers was one private corporation that led the field by starting child care centers back in 1979. They have licensing capacities for more than seventy children including infants.

Other corporations, such as IBM and Xerox, with employee bases of 20,000 or more employees, have chosen to assist their employees through enhanced referrals. (For details on enhanced referrals, see Chapter 7.) With the employer footing the bills for this service, new job opportunities are opening up for "Employee Child Care Specialists," people who are trained to work with families in obtaining suitable child care arrangements.

Religious-Related Child Care

Religious-related (church-related) child care programs are usually found in private, non-profit, church-sponsored facilities. The Heritage

Foundation states that more than half of all child care programs are housed in these facilities (CBS Sunday Morning Show, January 4, 1990).

Many of the church-related programs begun in the 1950s as part-day programs are still using the same child-oriented philosophies in their teaching methodology. Their curriculums not only include religious philosophy, they also stress socialization skills.

To meet the needs of today's working parents, many of these centers have changed their structures and operate twelve hours per day. Their programs usually emphasize personal attention and utilize child development points of view. Rather than offering impressive buildings, Sunday school rooms are used as classrooms.

Before applying for work at these schools, make sure you agree with the individual school's philosophy.

Montessori Schools

Montessori schools offer an education program with specialized learning methodology following guidelines as originally set up by Maria Montessori. Born in 1870 in Italy, Maria Montessori was the first woman in Italy to receive a medical degree. However, she is best known for her contributions to the education of young children. After finding successful approaches in working with retarded children, she founded the "Casa de Bambini" in 1907.

Theorizing that normal children, as well as retarded children, are greatly influenced by their environment, Montessori believed that children learn best through their five senses. Hence, this is the reason Montessori schools use sandpaper letters in teaching the alphabet.

Montessori designed her classrooms in an attractive child-size manner. The classroom equipment contains didactic materials to help children learn concepts. Children are taught to treat the equipment with care and respect. The equipment is displayed within easy reach of the children, so they can use it independently of the teacher.

Montessori schools were highly successful in Italy and throughout Europe in the 1920s and 1930s. The Association Montessori International is headquartered in the Netherlands. The Montessori schools became popular in the United States during the 1960s, and their influence continues today.

In the thirty-four states that require licensing, these schools must meet state regulations for ratios and room size. For more information about job opportunities in the Montessori schools, contact one of the following organizations:

ASSOCIATION MONTESSORI
    INT'L. U.S.A.
Houston Services Center
11230 Harwin Dr.
Houston, TX 77072

AMERICAN MONTESSORI
    SOCIETY INC.
150 Fifth Ave., Suite 203
New York, NY 10011

Parks and Recreation

Parks and recreation programs offer a variety of programs for non-working mothers such as "Mommy and Me" for new mothers and their infants and a "Tiny Tots" program for children ages three to five. Usually part-time programs, they operate two to three hours a day three times a week.

These programs provide socialization skills and arts and crafts for the young child. For the working parents, some parks and recreation programs offer after school care (extended care) for five to twelve year olds.

Many of these programs are not licensed by the state, so they provide good entry level positions for college students or child care workers who are seeking part-time work.

YMCA and YWCA Extended Day Care Programs

"Y" programs were instrumental in offering extended day care for the school-age child in the 1960s. Today, most of the Ys offer transportation to and from public school sites for children ages five to thirteen. Some of the Ys also offer on-site recreational activities for youngsters. These activities include swim lessons, field trips, and arts and crafts. Since the 1980s many of these programs have chosen to be regulated by their state's ratio standards.

You may need some recreational college course work to obtain employment with the Ys. College students find great opportunities with the Y programs because of the flexibility of hours.

For more information about YMCA programs, contact the following office:

YMCA of USA
101 N. Wacker Dr.
Chicago, IL 60606
(800) USA-YMCA

Cooperative Preschools

Cooperative preschools are private schools in which parents own a share of the school and hire a professional teacher or director to administer the program. Parents serve on the board and make the policy decisions. The parents are also responsible for the maintenance of the school.

Since most cooperative preschools are non-profit, parents usually pay a small fee and frequently serve as assistants to the paid staff. These schools are open on a part-time basis. For example, parents may send their child just two days a week. This type of school is popular with the non-working parent.

Private Preschool Program (Nursery School)

Similar in some ways to cooperative preschools, nursery schools are designed for children ages 2½ to 5 years. They are operated on a part-time basis, usually with a two to three hour morning program and a two to three hour afternoon program. Parents may choose to send their child two to five days per week. For example, a child may only attend Mondays, Wednesdays, and Fridays. These preschool programs are based on a development approach to curriculum.

This is an excellent job opportunity for those interested in part-time work.

A DAY IN THE LIFE OF A CHILD CARE DIRECTOR

As the director of a non-profit day care center, my day begins at 6:45 a.m. when I arrive to unlock the doors. Shortly before 7:00 a.m. an infant/toddler teacher and a preschool teacher arrive to help me greet the children and parents.

During the first 1½ hours, I work in an Infant/Toddler classroom where I have a chance to know the parents and children. Parents from the preschool side of the building also stop by on their way out if they have questions, requests, or concerns.

At 8:30 a.m. I go to my office on the preschool side of the building. During the next hour, my phone rings frequently, and a number of parents stop in to say hello. My door, located by the sign-in book, is usually open. By 9:30 a.m. most of the phone calls about attendance are over and the drop-in visits by parents have diminished.

For the next hour I usually attend to business details—writing receipts for that day's tuition payments, making out the deposit slip, and returning phone calls. Hopefully, by 10:30 a.m. I have finished with the morning essentials and can make the rounds of the classrooms. I like to get into all of the classrooms at least twice a day.

I try to spend time with each teacher and particularly some of the new children. It is during this time period I would schedule visits for new children entering school. I also direct the housekeeper to areas that may need a little extra cleaning attention, or put the floater to work on a special project such as book repairs. Prior to 11:30 a.m. I go over the lunch count and any supply orders with the housekeeper.

My phone rings frequently during the day. The biggest headache for most directors is finding substitutes for staff who call in sick. I'm fortunate not to have this headache; our teachers are rarely absent.

Many of my daily phone calls are from parents looking for child care. We're licensed for eighty children (sixty youngsters from two to five years of age and twenty infant/toddlers). Our waiting list runs in the 125-150 range. I refer parents who need immediate child care to a

Resource & Referral agency. I never refer them to any particular center.

I eat lunch at my desk, usually from 12:00 to 12:30 p.m. Once in a while I will run some errand off grounds or even shut my door and take a short nap.

The building is usually quiet between 1:00 and 3:00 p.m. During this time I have an opportunity to read articles and journals on child development issues. I also make a trip to the business office to drop off our deposit and pick up mail. Whenever necessary, I use this time period to work on special projects, budgets, long-range planning, or correspondence.

Our staff meetings are held monthly in two sessions (12:30 to 1:00 p.m. and 1:00 to 1:30 p.m.). We also handle the monthly in-service the same way. ("In-service" is on-the-job training for new and/or existing employees.)

Around 3:00 p.m. I try to visit the classrooms again, so the children can show me what they've done today. At this point I'm able to get an overview of how the day has gone. I make a mental note of any items that I want to discuss with an individual teacher privately.

Before leaving at 4:00 p.m., I check with the lead teachers of both the preschool and infant/toddler sides of the building. Although many directors end up taking work home, I never do.

A DAY IN THE LIFE OF A PRESCHOOL TEACHER

I work in a corporate preschool that has all the latest equipment, from a 3½ foot deep swimming pool to color-coordinated paint containers with matching lids. I couldn't want for anything more—other than better wages.

As a single mom raising two daughters, ages seven and three, I'm thankful this preschool offers a before and after school program for my eldest and a class for my youngest. I pay a small fee for these programs. However, I do have dental and medical benefits.

The parents who send their children to our preschool are generally middle class with both parents working. A one-half day program is also offered for parents who work part-time or stay home. No grants or government subsidies are offered here.

My team teacher and I have twenty-four children in our classroom, ranging in age from 3½ to 4 years old. It's a wonderful feeling to "click" with another teacher. Valerie and I have the same desires—the need to make life interesting, pleasurable, and fulfilling for our preschool youngsters.

When I arrive in the classroom at 8:15 a.m., the children are involved in the activities that interest them. A couple of youngsters may be enjoying the science table, which has a hamster, a bird, a magnifying glass, different rocks, and plants. Several may be in the drama play area where we have play dishes, a wooden sink, a stove and refrigerator, a child-size couch and chairs, and a dining room table.

One of the most popular areas is the "dress up" area where we have gaudy dresses, aprons, vests, hats, boots, high heels, purses, and eyeglass frames.

Justin is working out some of his anxieties of being a big brother by role-playing with dolls. Christopher is dressed up as Santa and is taking orders from his classmates. David has set up his own theater by rearranging some chairs so he can perform his version of a play.

During the day the children spend their longest moments in the art area where we have colored paper, pencils, scissors, crayons, paints, brushes, various collage materials and, of course, smocks for their "messy" creations.

Those with a creative flair like the block area. In fact, when Sam's parents were having a swimming pool built in his backyard, he duplicated this experience by building one for the school, complete with diving board and steps.

The math area contains puzzles, snap blocks, beads for stringing, and magnetic boards. Our last area is a listening area with a shelf for books, a phonograph for records, a tape player, and a flannel board for stories. The listening area is where we spend a lot of our time. During our sessions here, new ideas are explored, new brothers and sisters discussed, and death is openly shared. The time spent in the listening area makes my whole day worthwhile.

The preschool has designed three outdoor play areas with appropriate play equipment for different age groups plus a fenced-in swimming pool. The pool is used during the summer months under the supervision of a certified lifeguard. Everyone loves the pool.

We encourage personal responsibility that is age-appropriate. Here's how one problem is solved:

Joey knocks down Brian's high-rise. Brian is crying and Joey looks on gleefully. I take both boys by the hand, kneel down to their level, and ask, "What's happening?" The gleeful look on Joey's face turns to worry with Brian's accusations.

"Okay, so Joey came over here and kicked down your building. Is this correct?" I ask.

"Yes, but . . . he wouldn't let me play," Joey says.

I ask Joey to verbalize the main rule for the block area. "You build it, you knock it down," he says.

We talk about Brian's sadness and anger, then Brian says, "Hey Joey, you want to build a farm?"

I have successfully averted another crisis in a child's life. All part of a typical day in the life of a preschool teacher.

Preschool Teacher's Eight-Hour Schedule

Hours	Duties
7:30	Arrival—greet parents. Children arrange the room for breakfast. Children wash hands before breakfast.
8:00	Breakfast time; children assist the teacher and pass out food. Time to talk with children about food. Children help with the cleanup.
8:30	Group time; teacher shares the day's lesson; sing songs, read stories.
9:00	Cleanup and toilet time.
9:15	Outside play; supervised gross motor activity (climbing equipment, tricycles, sand box).
10:15	Snack time.
10:30	Inside time—learning center choices (dramatic play, blocks, arts, crafts, music).
11:30	Cleanup and toilet time.
11:45	Children assist teacher in setting up for lunch; children help pass out food; teacher discusses nutrition and/or new food introductions.
12:30	Nap time; teacher rubs backs, plays soft music; teachers usually use these two hours for their own lunch break and lesson preparations.
2:30	Nap time is over; teacher helps put on shoes; toilet time.
2:45	Snack time.
3:00	Outside free play time.
3:30	Teacher departs; children usually merge with other staff members until parents pick them up.

SALARIES AND BENEFITS

The 1989 Summary of Child Care Center Salaries, Benefits and Working Conditions, conducted by National Child Care Staffing Study (NCCSS), surveyed child care centers in Boston, Atlanta, Detroit, Phoenix, and Seattle. The study found that child care teachers are earning a low hourly wage of $5.35. The same study also concluded: despite the fact many child care teachers have high levels of formal education, they earn abysmally low wages; staff turnover in child care has nearly tripled in the last decade, jumping from 15 percent in 1977 to 41 percent in 1988; a shortage of trained child care teachers threatens the existing child care systems.

Some states, such as Hawaii, Colorado, and Illinois, have conducted similar surveys in collaboration with the Child Care Employee project. Their surveys also show low wages in the child care field—$6.25 in Hawaii, $4.67 in Colorado, and $4.79 in Illinois.

On most career tracks, benefits frequently help supplement earnings. However, in the child care field, few workers receive health and dental coverage, retirement benefits, or life insurance. Ironically, child care workers in the public sector do receive these benefits and usually twice the starting salary. (See Chapter 5 for details on these employment opportunities.) Reduced-fee child care is about the only benefit for child care teaching staff.

Another study conducted in the Southern California area in 1989 by Barbara Nicholls for the Foothill Affiliate of the Southern California Association for the Education of Young Children shows the following employee salaries:

Average Hourly Rate

Teachers
- Proprietary $6.82
- Nonprofit 8.46
- Public 8.61

Assistant Teachers
- Proprietary $5.05
- Nonprofit 5.99
- Public 6.22

Directors
- Proprietary $9.60
- Nonprofit 12.01
- Public 17.32

5. Public Sector Jobs

To understand how the government became involved in child care, you first have to be familiar with the roles that war, legislation, and federal and state funding played in developing child care standards.

A LEGISLATIVE HISTORY OF EARLY CHILDHOOD EDUCATION

Chronology of Important Events

1820s—Slightly more than 150 years ago an active movement, based on the English system of education, started in this country. Still known today as "Infant Schools," they were established to care for the children of immigrant mothers who needed to work in order to survive.

1854—The first day care center was established in a New York City hospital. When previously hospitalized mothers returned to work, they left their infants in the care of the nurses.

1898—The National Federation of Day Nurseries was founded. Within two years 175 centers were organized in cities across the United States. One of the original nursery schools is still operating today in Long Beach, California.

1912—The Department of Health, Education and Welfare established a Children's Bureau. Although licensing standards were set up for children's institutions, no funding was provided for child care services.

1930—A few California nursery school projects were funded under the Works Progress Administration during the Depression. In 1934 some 650 centers were in operation across the nation. Yet during this depression period, the government spent over $3 million on child care services for approximately 300,000 children.

1940s—Realizing that women would have to join the work force when the men went off to World War II, the government allocated the first federal funding for child care services. Congress passed a bill known as the Lanham Act. Established on school district sites, day care centers opened in thirty-nine states in 1943. California is one of the few states that still operates children's centers in public schools. The Santa

Monica School District and the Covina Valley School District in California are two of the original centers operating today. With federal funds, day care resources were made available to cities that couldn't otherwise support a center of their own.

1964—The "War on Poverty" included the theory that education was a solution to poverty.

1965 — In response to the government's commitment to offer Early Childhood Education to children from families in poverty, the Head Start program was started.

1969—The Department of Health, Education and Welfare added an Office of Child Development, thereby initiating a comprehensive approach to the development of young children.

1970-78—The Administration of Children, Youth and Families (ACYF) of the Department of Health, Education and Welfare made a commitment to bringing quality to child care by initiating the CDA credential. (In 1985 NAEYC entered into agreement with ACYF to assume management of this program.) The CDA credential is frequently a requirement for employment in government programs such as Head Start.

1978 — Title XX-Social Service funds for child care were increased. California received $20 million, using $12.2 million to expand child care services.

1980—The Department of Health and Human Services proposed day care regulations for setting standards such as staff ratios, training qualifications, and health care for children. These regulations were adopted but never implemented.

You now understand the major roles federal and state governments play in funding child care. In 1988 federal child care assistant programs and Head Start programs received $6.9 billion. Although this may sound like a lot of money, these funds have little effect on child care for today's working parents.

Head Start, for example, is a part-time program at best, only three hours daily and only for four year olds in most states. Yet this isn't the answer for the working poor who need full-time care for at least ten hours daily. New legislation, such as the Act for Better Child Care, may make Head Start a full-time program.

The flurry of recent attention to child care is a direct result of new trends in the work force. Child care in the past was a social or welfare issue, but currently with 65 percent of all working women having children under six years of age, child care has become an issue that demands government recognition and action.

The American public supports a stronger governmental role in helping families find quality and affordable child care while upgrading compensation for child care workers. During future election years, child care issues are sure to be in the forefront.

The Act for Child Care

In November 1987 the Act for Child Care was introduced in Congress by Senator Chris Dodd. The original bill authorized $2.1 billion for child care, covering such areas as:

- Full day care for Head Start children.
- Early childhood programs and school-age programs for centers located on school sites.
- Services for infants, toddlers, and young children through community-based centers and family day care homes.
- Training and support services to public and private providers.
- Development of model program standards.
- Dependent care tax credit.

In the spring of 1990, this bill had passed both the Senate and the House and was sent to the President for his signature. In the fall of 1990, the bill was passed under the name, "Child Care and Development Block Grant." The challenge, of course, will be to ensure that this bill serves the long-term needs of America's children, not simply the election needs of politicians.

HEAD START PROGRAM

Head Start is one of the most successful federal ECE programs ever developed. It was designed to help break the cycle of poverty by providing preschool children of low-income families with a comprehensive program to meet the children's emotional, social, health, nutritional, and psychological needs.

Head Start provided a unique type of child care educational program by emphasizing parental support and involvement. Although funded by the federal government, the program is locally administered by some 1,500 community-based, non-profit organizations and public school systems. Grants are awarded by the Health and Human Services regional offices.

Eight Major Components to the Head Start Program

1. **Education**: Designed to meet each child's individual needs, Head Start is known to choose quality curriculums such as High/Scope®, a curriculum presently enacted in many communities throughout the United States. Head Start also aims to meet the ethnic and cultural characteristics of the community it serves.

2. **Special Needs Children**: Because Head Start programs have low child/staff ratios, the teachers learn to work with handicapped

children. Ten percent of all children who enter this program have some type of diagnosed handicap — blindness, hearing problems, learning disabilities, or mental retardation, for example.

3. **Health Services**: Head Start emphasizes the importance of identifying health problems early. Many preschool children from low income families have never seen a doctor or dentist, so Head Start makes these services available.

4. **Nutrition**: In order to meet at least one-third of each child's daily nutritional needs, children are served one hot meal and one snack daily.

5. **Parental Involvement**: Believing that parents are the most important influence in a child's development, Head Start operates under the premise that children will learn best if their families are involved in the program. Each parent is asked to volunteer once every two weeks in his or her child's classroom. Policy Council Committees, which are made up of parents, have strong voices in the administrative and managerial decisions.

6. **Social Services**: Designed to help families assess their needs, the Head Start program provides services to meet these needs. Social workers help families with crisis intervention, food, and clothing whenever the need arises.

7. **Mental Health**: Mental health professionals, such as psychologists, are available to provide training to staff and parents. These professionals help parents recognize the importance of getting help early when their children have problems.

8. **Administration**: The key person in making a Head Start program function well is the administrator. Judy Sanders, Head Start Administrator for fifteen programs, shares some of her duties:

- Determining which services should be provided for her particular parents and children as outlined by the delegating agency.
- Providing leadership for setting overall goals and objectives as a basis for the curriculum.
- Directing staff in day-to-day operation of the program.
- Ensuring that state licensing standards are met.
- Establishing a method of hearing and resolving community concerns and complaints about the program.
- Providing leadership for parental involvement and education.
- Taking responsibility for the entire budget, preparing a year-end analysis of the budget and expenditures. Applying for government grants and state funding.
- Procuring classroom locations.

Salaries

Head Start teachers can expect to make $8 to $12 per hour. (Head

Start is a ten-month program in most states and not funded for the summer months.) Although usually a six-hour position, some programs have one three-hour morning program and another three-hour afternoon program.

Directors generally make $35,000 to $55,000. Salaries are determined by the funding source. Salaries vary, depending upon the geographical or regional location of the program.

CALIFORNIA'S CHILD CARE SYSTEM

"California has the best funded and most comprehensive child care and development system in the nation. Program funding, amounting to approximately $332 million, is comparable to that of all other states combined and surpasses many industrial nations. California's program results from legislative and community advocacy spanning fifty years."

State Department Child Development
Program Facts 1988-1989

According to Dr. Robert Cervantes, Director of the Child Development Division of the California State Department of Education (SDE), these programs are designed and funded to serve the "working poor."

As a job seeker, you will find the following information about California's State Department of Education programs helpful in your pursuit of a child care career.

General Subsidized Child Care

These programs, which serve infants through thirteen years of age, are required to provide age-appropriate curriculum and activities, a nutritional program, parental counseling, and referrals. Families are placed on a waiting list. It may take one or two years before a family receives services. Fees for the families are on a sliding scale based on income. Families receiving welfare payments are not charged for this program.

Generally, these programs are operated by school districts and county offices of education. However, some are operated by local community action organizations and some by private, proprietary, and nonprofit corporations.

Job opportunities in these programs are usually found in the larger school districts, such as Los Angeles and Sacramento, which employ approximately 900 child development teachers, or Pomona Unified School District, which employs approximately 150 child care people.

Depending on the geographical location, teachers in California subsidized children's centers earn from $22,000 to $32,000 annually.

Campus Child Development

Campus programs are primarily for the children of students enrolled in college and frequently serve as a "hands-on" classroom experience for students enrolled in child development classes. The centers are operated either by student associations or by the administration offices.

Contact your local Resource & Referral agency for a listing of community colleges in your area that have such programs. California's Community College Chancellor has a goal of providing child care programs on all 107 campuses. Salary ranges will differ, since not all college campus programs are currently being funded by SDE.

Teacher positions earn $8 to $15 per hour, while director positions have a salary range of $25,000 to $40,000.

Alternative Payment Program

This program is designed to pay child care expenses for low-income families in which the parents are working or going to school. As a vendor/voucher program, parents have a choice in child care, either in a day care center or in a family day care home. The monthly voucher payment is made directly to the child care provider.

Respite Care

As short-term care, this program is designed to help families who are under stress due to medical or emotional problems or who are going through difficult transitions and need relief. Children who are at risk of abuse or are abused must be referred by legal, medical, social service, or other community agencies. This program serves children from birth through thirteen years of age. Usually, families are helped for three months only.

State Preschool Program

This developmental preschool program for children ages three to five includes parent education and participation as well as health, nutrition, and social services for children and their families. Some programs are bilingual. Only low income families are eligible, and abused or neglected children have top priority.

Public Administrator Positions in California

Administrative positions will become more and more common during the 1990s as the child care field gains attention. Presently, these administrative positions comprise less than three percent of the openings. Similar to the chief executive officer of a large corporation, many of you will want to complete your education and training in order to achieve this position.

Bill Ewing, an administrator for Pomona Unified School District, one of California's largest school districts, works with a child care budget of approximately $4 million. Funded by contracts with the State Department of Education/Child Development Division, he oversees such areas as the children's center programs, infant programs, Resource & Referral agency programs, extended day programs, alternative payment programs, state preschool, and respite care programs. Head Start, a federally funded program, is also under Ewing's direction.

According to Ewing, the responsibilities of being an administrator are almost beyond enumerating, but here are some of the highlights:

Fiscal
- Develop budgets for each type of program.
- Complete annual non-competitive applications for funds.
- Approve all agreements with subcontractors and submit for school district approval.

Implementation of Regulations
- Ensure that families are eligible to receive services.
- Implement licensing requirements of Title 5 and the Community Care Licensing.
- Make certain that attendance/enrollment records are being maintained according to law.

Legal
- Have a working knowledge and operate various programs according to Education Code, child development guidelines, child development funding terms and conditions, Head Start regulations, State Board of Controls regulations, child care food regulations, California School Accounting manual, State of California Department of Social Services Community Care Licensing.

Personnel
- Recruit, interview, hire, and evaluate staff.
- Make recommendations to the District Representative negotiation sessions following a study of the income, the proposal from the certificated or classified bargaining unit, and the costs associated with implementing the request.

Educational/Community/Advocacy
- Develop appropriate educational programs for infants through school-age children.
- Implement the State Program Quality Review and publicize the program to the public.
- Keep current on legislation; help write legislation; work with elected officials.

Parents/Children
- Develop a parent handbook; form a parent advisory group;

- meet with individual parents to resolve problems and concerns.
- Provide for the social, intellectual, nutritional, safety, and health needs of the children.

Site Facility Management
- Be responsible for multiple child care locations.
- Coordinate facility sharing with principals and other administrators.
- Develop and gain school board approval for the program's goals.
- Represent the programs at workshops planned by the State Department of Education and County Office of Nutrition.

Depending on individual school districts, bargaining contracts and funding sources, most administrators in California have the salary equivalency of a senior high school principal—$50,000 to $65,000 annually.

6. Other Potential Job Opportunities

Only recently have middle and upper class Americans shown an increased interest in pursuing child care careers. In the past, pay was notoriously low, training was limited, and the chances for advancement were remote. Today, the picture is changing. The typical child care worker is more educated and better paid, and has greater prospects for advancement in this career.

THE CHANGING PICTURE OF CHILD CARE

People who are interested in continuing their education and broadening their work experience will find themselves on the doorstep to new opportunities in the child care field. In positions working directly with children, you will make a direct impact on their lives; in some positions you will indirectly affect the lives of children; and in many new and exciting positions, you can play a vital role in shaping national policies regarding our youngsters, today as well as in the future.

Let's explore these paths in the world of child care.

NANNIES

Just within the last decade, nanny training programs have opened the doors to an adventuresome career, some with the nation's "rich and famous." Most working parents opt for a day care home or center, but other high-income, dual career families like the idea of an old-fashioned, live-in nanny. Child Care Resource and Referral agencies report that 20 percent of their phone requests are for nannies. The demand for U.S.-trained nannies is growing faster than the supply. Schools for training nannies are located in several cities across the nation. The training fees vary from school to school, with many offering their services as placement agencies.

The trained nanny is hired as either a live-in or live-out caregiver for preschool children in a family. She or he is responsible for the total well-being of each child. Nannies don't work as maids or housekeepers, and they never do windows! Instead, nannies help teach, toilet train, discipline, play with, read to, rock, and most of all, love the children in their care.

Nannies are given a salary and usually room and board. Some families provide a car, health insurance, and paid vacations.

Before considering a nanny career, ask yourself a couple of questions: Do I enjoy children enough to be with them around the clock? Would I like living with another family?

Duties

Here is a list of some of the duties generally required of the nanny:
- Cuddling and diapering infants.
- Sterilizing bottles and preparing formula.
- Taking care of a sick child and giving medication as prescribed by the physician.
- Preparing meals, feeding the child, and washing their dishes.
- Bathing and grooming the child.
- Laundering the child's clothing.
- Keeping the nursery and play areas clean.
- Designing age-appropriate games and play activities, both indoors and outdoors.
- Reading stories and playing games with the child.
- Planning the child's birthday parties.
- Organizing trips to the zoo, park, museum, and other places of interest.
- Caring for a child twenty-four hours a day if the parents are out of town.
- Developing good interpersonal relations with the mother and/or father.

Working Conditions

Most nannies are employed by middle or upper class families. Some work for celebrities and vacation with the children and their families in exotic spots around the world.

Some nannies are hired on a day-to-day basis; others are hired as live-ins. Nannies usually work fifty to sixty hours in a five-day work week with weekends and holidays off.

As a nanny you should ask for a written contract that states your wages, Social Security deductions, paid holidays, and number of sick days allowed. All employers must pay your Social Security. Some states also require employers to pay worker's compensation and unemployment insurance.

Wages

Salaries for trained nannies range from $165 per week to $400 per week, depending on the family, the number of children, your education and experience, and the other benefits included. A recent survey in southern California indicated that the average starting salary was $1,200 per month with room and board included.

CHILD CARE CONSULTANTS

Successful consultants in the child care field come from a myriad of backgrounds, according to Barbara Berg, one highly successful child care consultant. These backgrounds include Resource & Referral management, college instruction, business management, and active on-site child care experience.

The ideal consultant combines his or her expertise in business management with human resource training and child care experience. People who have operated a child care center generally possess the right qualifications to become a freelance consultant. Some of these skills include being a facilitator of workshops on child care issues; developing and managing budgets for a variety of programs; and interfacing with business and government agencies.

If you are realistic, good at interacting, and know how to interface with people whose needs often conflict, then child care consulting may be the right job for you.

Preparing Yourself

Don't leave your present job until you are in a solid financial position. It takes time to sell your services as a consultant. You will be selling your expertise and services to businesses, government agencies, and private corporations. You will be communicating with and educating corporate decision-makers about your services.

Don't burn bridges at your old job. You may need to make use of your past contacts.

Consultants are called upon for their expertise. Develop your knowledge of tax laws, liability issues, and state and local licensing regulations. Make sure you have a working knowledge of legal/contractual issues pertaining to child care. Familiarize yourself with all types of child care payment systems.

Some consultants specialize in certain areas of child care. Barbara, for example, specializes in offering presentations to employee groups on "Balancing Work and Family." Dennis Hudson, another consultant, handles feasibility studies for employers and business groups who want to open new centers.

Dennis suggests that aspiring consultants be prepared to work with both private and public clients. Two big differences exist between these two types of clients—the availability of grant monies and the difference in attitudes.

As an example, several California cities recently received one-time only grant monies to hire consultants for needs assessment, feasibility analysis, and data interpretation. Although private corporations use these same services, their attitudes about child care may be different. Rather than seeing the broad picture of child care, the corporation usually views it from other perspectives, such as setting up a consortium of local businesses to develop a day care center or providing a center for sick children only. As a consultant, you will need to understand all the various child care possibilities.

Wages

Consulting fees vary in different parts of the country and in accordance with the types of services involved. Some consultants charge by the hour, others by the project or presentation. Beginning consultants generally charge lower fees, around $50 per hour, until they become established.

For those of you with an entrepreneurial spirit, this challenging job as a consultant can open up new doors to success.

CHILD CARE COORDINATORS

During the past five years, an up-and-coming child care administrative position as a child care coordinator has developed for qualified individuals. To meet public demand for child care services, cities across the nation are taking a pro-active stand in creating day care centers for employers, promoting the expansion of quality child care programs, creating partnerships in child care programs, providing resource programs, and planning land use for child care facilities. Child care coordinators are needed to manage such programs.

Small City and Big City Opportunities

Most major child care programs are developed in the larger cities; however, some of today's smaller cities are also hiring child care coordinators. As an example, the small community of San Dimas in California, with a population of approximately 30,000, recently hired a full-time child care coordinator.

Educational requirements for small city and big city coordinators generally differ. Many small city coordinators find employment with an AA (two-year) degree, while big city coordinators usually need a BA Degree in Public Administration, Early Childhood Education, Social Welfare, or a related field. Positions in the larger cities will also require experience—four years as a director of an ECE program; community service directly related to child care; or advocacy or consultant work in a child care service agency.

Duties

Duties as a city child care coordinator may include, but are not limited to, the following:

- Activities that promote the expansion of accessible, affordable, and quality child care services.
- Preparing and disseminating a resource handbook to the public.
- Preparing a booklet on facility requirements for day care — planning, construction, fire/safety, business taxes, and licensing.
- Planning and staging child care fairs.
- Producing a directory of child care options for the city to distribute to the community.
- Facilitating a child care advisory board.

Kathy Malaske-Samu, Child Care Coordinator for Los Angeles County, a governmental agency employing some 80,000 people, has designed several innovative child care benefits for the work force. These programs include a flexible benefit plan, on-site child care, and alternative work schedules.

Wages

With more mothers entering into the paid labor force, many employers are compelled to rethink their benefit packages. For this reason, many cities are hiring coordinators to show employers that providing quality child care helps them retain employees.

Salaries differ from city to city across the nation. In general, you can expect to make $20,000 to $55,000, depending on the size of the city.

CHILD CARE INSTRUCTORS/ EDUCATORS/TEACHERS

Leadership and organizational skills are important qualifications for becoming a child care instructor. If you possess these skills, this job can be satisfying and financially secure.

Adult instructors affect the lives of children, albeit in a roundabout way. While a child care teacher is involved in the lives of approximately twenty-five children per semester, an adult instructor affects the lives of fifty adults per semester, who in turn will have an impact on the lives of some 1,500 children.

College Instructor

Joanna Jones exemplifies many of the people who are choosing to become early childhood educators. Because she was especially interested in educational research and curriculum writing, Joanna decided she could best influence the ECE field by becoming a college instructor. If you are interested in working with adults and have a desire to complete your college education, this position promises a lifelong career.

The responsibilities of a college early childhood instructor are varied. Most full-time instructors are required to teach three to four classes each semester with an additional two or three hours of preparation time required for each class. They are also responsible for spending one hour in their office each day. In addition to participating in the Faculty Senate, most instructors chair at least one school committee. Additionally, they are active in peer organizations that promote quality child care, affordability of child care, and better compensation for child care workers.

Jean Cohn, a child care college instructor at a community college, believes that instructing a class in Nursery School Administration is the perfect step in becoming a "super" director. As an instructor, Jean plans a yearly conference on campus for community day care directors who want to increase their knowledge of current child care practices and concerns.

California, one state with more than 107 community colleges, recently established new educational requirements. Prospective college instructors now need an M.A. Degree. Check with your state's Department of Education for educational requirements.

Part-time instructors can expect to make $29 to $32 per hour. Full-time instructors usually receive an annual salary between $30,000 and $60,000, depending on regional and state funding sources.

Vocational Instructor

If you have been working in the child care field for a minimum of five years and want to make a career change from working with children to teaching high school students, vocational instruction may be the career for you. Regional occupational instructors (vocational instructors) train high school students and adults for entry level positions in the field of child care. The goal is to teach child care competencies sufficiently well so your students become employable. Instructors also place their students in community child care programs for on-the-job training.

Pattie Marhoefer, a regional occupation instructor, says she gains a great deal of satisfaction from her job. Not only does she enjoy teaching, she also feels a sense of satisfaction in producing students who will bring quality to the child care field.

Vocational instructors are responsible for training students in: introduction to child care education, responsibilities of a child care worker, emergency care and basic first aid training, child development, curriculum development, psychology in the classroom, and attitudes and behaviors appropriate to a child care worker.

Educational requirements for this position are five years of teaching or directing an ECE program and nine units of course work at an accredited college.

The need for vocational instructors will continue to increase during the next few years as the government continues to pass new bills in support of vocational training.

Parent-Child Educator

In most states the position of parent-child educator comes under the auspices of local school districts and their Adult Education programs. Requirements vary, with each state setting its own standards. For example, in Minnesota, the parent-child educator needs a BA Degree in Early Childhood Education, while in California, you only need a Designated Subject Credential. (Requirements for a Designated Subject Credential are five years of documented experience in the field and college course work.)

Your duties involve working with parents and their children. As an example, for a three-hour class that meets four times a week, half of the time is spent in the classroom with the parents and their infants/toddlers or preschool children. The remaining time is spent with the parents to discuss child growth and development and the concerns of parenting.

Salaries vary from state to state, but $18 to $25 per hour is the usual range.

OTHER CHILD CARE ALTERNATIVES
Special Education Teacher

In effect since 1975, Public Law 94-1421 is considered the most significant piece of legislation for meeting the needs of handicapped children from ages 3 to 21. Public and county schools with special education departments are always looking for teachers who have credentials in special learning difficulties. Some of these learning difficulties include hearing impairment, developmental disabilities, and vision impairment. Teachers who enjoy enriching the lives of these children will find that there is high demand, as well as personal enrichment, for this type of sensitive teaching.

Duties for special education teaching include setting individualized educational goals for each student in your class. Class sizes are small, usually from 7 to 12 children. The duties may include lifting, toileting, and feeding developmentally disabled children and young adults.

Teachers in this special category can expect to earn salaries comparable to an elementary teacher or higher.

Child Life Specialist

Child life specialists perform a special function in the overall picture of child care careers. They are employed to meet the emotional and developmental needs of children receiving medical care and to help their families make positive adjustments to the illness or disability. These positions are found in major hospitals across the nation.

One child life specialist shares the duties of her position:

- Arranging the hospital-based playroom to meet the varying ages of pediatric patients.
- Creating appropriate arts and crafts activities.
- Role-playing as doctor and/or nurse to help children understand their illnesses or disabilities.
- Working with parents on age-appropriate activities for home and bed.
- Facilitating discussions with parents whose children have life-threatening diseases.

Child life specialists can expect to start their careers at a salary of $12 to $15 per hour.

Several colleges and universities offer child life specialist programs. Following are two California colleges offering studies in this program:

UNIVERSITY OF LAVERNE
1350 Third St.
LaVerne, CA 91750
(714) 593-3511

MILLS COLLEGE
5000 MacArthur Blvd.
Oakland, CA 94609
(415) 420-2255

For more information about schools and job opportunities, write:

THE ASSOCIATION FOR THE CARE OF CHILDREN'S HEALTH
3516 Wisconsin Ave. NW
Washington, DC 20016

Playground Worker

Both private and public schools employ part-time adults to assist teachers in supervising large groups of children on the playgrounds. These positions usually require some knowledge of age-appropriate activities for school-age children. This job is perfect for mothers who want to work the same hours and days that their children are in school.

Playground workers can expect to make minimum wage or be placed on the classified school district salary schedule as a teacher's aide.

Camp Counselor (Day or Residential)

Teenagers over the age of sixteen and other young adults may find enjoyable summer employment as camp counselors. Summer camps are sponsored by such organizations as Boy Scouts, Girl Scouts, Campfire, YMCA, and Jewish groups.

For employment with these youngsters, you'll need a knowledge of the developmental stages of children and age-appropriate activities.

Pay as a summer counselor is usually minimum wage. Residential counselors also receive room and board.

OTHER INTERESTING CHILD CARE SPECIALTIES

Child Care Ombudsman

In 1984 the California State Legislature created a Child Care Ombudsman Program to provide a link between day care licensing and the community. Although at this time the job opportunity is available only in California, other states give indication of establishing their own programs in the near future. Following are the responsibilities of the ombudsman as mandated by the legislature:

- Provide information to the public and parents on child day care licensing.
- Serve as liaison to business and labor, law enforcement, education, and child care providers.
- Disseminate information on the state's licensing role.
- Act as liaison to Child Care Resource & Referral agencies (CCR&Rs).
- Assist in the coordination of complaints and concerns on behalf of children in day care.

As a state position, the salary ranges from $35,000 to $45,000, depending on experience. For up-to-date information about this program, contact:

STATE OMBUDSMAN HEADQUARTERS
744 P St., MS 19-62
Sacramento, CA 95814
(916) 324-4038

Sales Representative for Suppliers of Child Care Materials

For those interested in sales work, many excellent opportunities are available with suppliers of quality educational and child care materials. Following are the names, addresses, and phone numbers of five of the largest suppliers:

LAKESHORE
2695 E. Dominguez
Carson, CA 90749
(800) 421-5354

BECKLEY-CARDY
129 Gaither, Suite M
Mt. Laurel, NJ 08054
(800) 227-1178

CHILDCRAFT
20 Kilmen Rd.
Edison, NJ 08813
(800) 631-6100

KAPLAN
P.O. Box 609
Lewisville, NC 27023
(800) 334-2014

CONSTRUCTIVE PLAYTHINGS
1227 East 119th St.
Grandview, MO 64030
(816) 761-5900

If you decide on this career opportunity, companies such as Childcraft require that their sales representatives have an educational and work background in Early Childhood Education. Sales reps frequently give presentations or serve as workshop leaders at ECE conferences. Other responsibilities include being able to give cost breakdowns per child for age-appropriate materials and being knowledgeable about licensing requirements to help set up classroom learning materials.

If you are an energetic "people" person who can manage a base-salary with commissions, this position can be exciting and lucrative.

Author/Illustrator

Many children's book authors and/or illustrators are self-employed; however, parents' magazines, child care trade journals, and publishing houses occasionally offer full-time employment. In creating stories for a specific age group, you'll need knowledge of children's developmental levels. Once your knowledge of age-appropriate materials and activities becomes useful within the industry, you will be considered an expert.

Miscellaneous Career Ideas

Numerous other career options provide excellent opportunities for working with children, families, businesses, or combinations of all three. Many require specialized schooling; others do not. Here's a list of ideas and suggestions for your consideration:

Children's Librarian
Dance Instructor
Child Psychologist
Child Psychiatrist
Child Life Specialist in the
　health care field
Pediatrician
Dental Hygienist

Pediatric Dentist
Drama Teacher
Swimming Instructor
Pediatric Nurse
Children's Store Owner
Licensed Social Evaluator of
　Child Care Centers

7. Child Care Resource & Referral Agencies

> **WANTED**
> **RESOURCE AND REFERRAL WORKER**
> Position open for Child Care Broker, Social Worker, Legislative Analyst, Child Care Advocate, Data Collector, Demographer, Disseminator of Information, Telemarketer, Money Manager, Computer Specialist, Child Care Specialist. Everything to Everyone. Only high energy applicants need apply. Call today for an interview.

America's need for child care has risen dramatically in the last decade. According to statistics, more than 25 million children ages thirteen and under are being cared for in a variety of child care settings while their parents work. On the supply side of the picture, child care services have proliferated, looking much like a patchwork quilt made up of public and private programs. Statistics show as many as 63,000 day care centers and 165,000 day care homes across the nation.

Today, working parents, regardless of their income levels, share the common problem of finding a child care program that meets their particular needs. This search for child care can be difficult and stressful.

Not only is adequate quality child care a concern for parents, but public officials, business leaders, employers, and community leaders now are realizing that child care is a much-needed service in their communities. Yet, oftentimes there's no resource for getting a clear picture of what child care involves, what the parents are looking for, and what services are available.

In response to this growing need, Child Care Resource and Referral (CCR&R) programs began emerging and evolving twelve years ago. Today, over 270 of these programs exist in the United States. They are funded by local, state, or federal monies and are considered nonprofit agencies. Most services are free to the parents and community. However, many newly established CCR&R programs are charging for their services.

ALL ABOUT CCR&R SERVICES

The CCR&R agency is a true timesaver for parents and the community. The major services performed by CCR&R agencies include assisting parents in their child care search, using methods that promote parental choice, and maintaining documentation of parents' requests for services. The CCR&R agency is a resource for governmental and public requests for several types of statistics:

- Number of calls/contracts for child care referrals
- Ages of children needing care
- Hours of care needed
- Requests for special hours (nights, weekends, shifts)
- Reasons for child care requests (working, school, respite)

The CCR&R agency develops, maintains, and prepares quarterly updates of a resource file of basic information on each of the providers, including type of program, hours of service, ages served, fees and eligibility, and program information. Existing child care providers include:

- Licensed family day care homes
- Licensed public and private child care centers, preschools, and nursery schools
- Full-time and part-time programs
- Infant, preschool, and school-age programs

Technical assistance is provided by the agency to existing and potential child care providers in such areas as start-up and licensing procedures/regulations; resources and general information; updates on recent issues in child care/child development; and facilitating communications among child care programs and child-related services on the local level.

The major services of a CCR&R agency are provided at the local level in a variety of ways—monthly or bimonthly newsletters; written information on choosing child care, such as brochures and checklists; workshops for child care providers on special issues such as tax information, child abuse prevention, and infant/child development; and immediate on-line telephone referral service to parents and walk-ins. Many CCR&R agencies also have toy and lending library programs.

Job Banks

Many agencies also provide job banks as a community service. These are handled through one of the counselors. Essentially, job banks coordinate available positions in Child Development and Early Childhood Education with qualified individuals seeking employment. Anyone with a job opening in Child Development or Early Childhood Education may list the position with the job bank. Individuals looking for a job in the field may contact the job bank.

For a list of CCR&R agencies that have job banks, contact the National Association of Child Care Referral Agencies. (See address at the end of this chapter.)

COUNSELOR/REFERRAL WORKERS

As a CCR&R counselor, you will help parents make child care choices by providing them with information. You will also provide information to the community about marketing child care, as well as child care statistics, licensing, and local ordinances. In large agencies there may be 10 to 20 referral specialists.

Some counselors only help parents connect with child care; other counselor positions are not so easily defined. Following are some of the other areas of responsibility:

- Employer-related parent requests
- Family day care recruitment
- Technical assistance to prospective day care center operators
- Technical assistance to existing day care providers
- Managing the lending library or toy loans
- Visits to child care programs
- Collecting data on child care providers
- Parental counseling (options for parents; consumer education; handling difficult situations; telephone interviews with parents)

The responsibilities assigned to a particular counselor are determined by the agency's funding level. In a small agency, the counselor may have to perform all of these duties. Job opportunities for CCR&R counselors include: Child Care Resource & Referral Agencies, corporate personnel departments, employee assistance programs, human services agencies, community agencies such as mental health and welfare assistance programs, Work-Family Directions, Inc. and Partnership Group, Inc.

CALIFORNIA'S CHILD CARE PROGRAMS FOR LOW INCOME FAMILIES

Although the following information concerns California programs, check with your state's Department of Social Services for similar subsidy programs.

One of the unique aspects of CCR&R programs in California is that they are "everything to everybody." They service all families and providers regardless of income or other eligibilities, and they serve as an important resource for governmental agencies and businesses.

Many California CCR&R agencies receive state and federal monies to fund child care programs for low-income and/or welfare families. Three of these programs are Alternative/Payment Program, Respite Care Program, and GAIN.

Alternative/Payment Program

Also called the "Vendor/Voucher" program, this unique program was designed to accommodate qualified parents who have unusual work schedules. Children who are abused, neglected, or at risk are first in priority to receive services. Next to qualify for services are the lowest income families who are working or are in training programs. The sliding fee scale for child care is considerably lower than in the private sector. The program serves children of all ages. The person handling this program is called an Alternative Payment Clerk or Alternative Payment Manager.

Respite Care Program

The respite care program is a short-term program designed to help families who are under stress either because of medical or emotional problems or because of difficult transitions. Abused or at-risk children must have a referral from a legal, medical, or social service agency. Within many CCR&R agencies, this job is an additional responsibility for the Alternative Payment Manager. No fee is charged for the services rendered.

Greater Avenues for Independence (GAIN)

Recently, the government has sponsored several welfare reform programs for families receiving Aid to Families of Dependent Children (AFDC) funds to help them move toward economic independence. Across the nation the Family Support Act of 1988 (FSA) is presently being implemented.

In support of the FSA, the GAIN program has attracted the attention of California Child Care Resource & Referral agencies. These agencies are contributing their child care expertise to assist parents who are searching for child care.

Recognizing that most welfare recipients want to work if they have the opportunity, GAIN provides that opportunity through education, job training, and job placement. Child care is one of the supportive services paid for by the GAIN program. Child care costs for any child under age twelve are paid for by the county welfare department for GAIN participants. The CCR&R agency usually contracts with the welfare department to provide child care referrals.

Each county writes its own program for approval by the state. The aim is to find unsubsidized employment for each person in the GAIN. Participants stay in the program until that aim is achieved.

CHILD CARE FOOD PROGRAM

Established by Congress in 1968, the Child Care Food Program is available to most child care centers and family day care homes across the nation. Recognizing that proper nutritional and eating habits are essential to the psychological and physical well-being of children, funds for the program are established by Congress and disbursed to umbrella agencies.

These umbrella agencies, usually nonprofit organizations, may apply to their state government's Office of Nutrition to receive these funds. The rates that the government reimburses child care providers are effective from July 1 to June 30. (The current rates are listed in Chapter 7.)

Also, many food sponsors are private and not affiliated with CCR&R agencies. Call your local CCR&R agency for the names of other sponsors who may have Food Monitor positions. Career-minded individuals with a nutritional background may find their niche in this position.

EMPLOYER-RELATED SERVICES

In the field of employer-supported child care services, enhanced or customized referrals are one of the fastest growing trends in the workplace. This trend will continue to grow as more employers add child care benefits. In fact, many experts predict that child care benefits will be as commonplace as retirement plans by 1995. The number of companies giving child care assistance to employees grew from 100 companies in 1978 to nearly 3,500 in 1987.

Employer-related services, such as enhanced-referrals, are a growing trend. Two major organizations currently have direct contracts with large employee-based corporations—Work/Family Directions, Inc. and Partnership Group, Inc. These organizations provide consultation to corporations and businesses. They strive to create a partnership among employers, working parents, and child care providers. They also advocate child care legislation and produce a wide range of materials and videos designed specifically for working parents. They assist companies in designing and administering customized systems to help employees pay for child care.

For more information about these employer-related services, write or call:

WORK/FAMILY DIRECTIONS, INC.
930 Commonwealth Ave. South
Boston, MA 02215-1212
(617) 566-1800

PARTNERSHIP GROUP, INC.
National Resource Center
840 Main St.
Lansdale, PA 19446
(800) VIP-KIDS

Here's how the service works with the CCR&R agencies:

Nationwide companies, such as IBM, Xerox, Allstate, and Johnson & Johnson to name a few, contract with CCR&R agencies for child care services for their employees. Many CCR&R counselors make direct contracts with local employers.

The employee is given an 800 number to help locate one of the 270 CCR&R agencies. The agency in turn calls a referral counselor who is familiar with the child care data base in their locale. As a child care expert, the designated counselor will help the parent identify his/her child care needs and discuss the available options. The referral counselor, who works as a child care broker, calls in advance to verify openings with local child care providers.

As a truly customized service, the counselor makes follow-up calls to the parent to make sure the child care arrangements are satisfactory.

Companies with an employee base of 1,500 or more commonly work with CCR&Rs. Since this is a growing trend with large employers, a few CCR&R agencies hire a dedicated employee-related counselor to work on this service.

CCR&R JOB OPPORTUNITIES AND REQUIREMENTS

If your attitude tends to be melioristic, meaning that you feel your purpose is to make this world a better place, you'll find that child care careers will satisfy this need. Following are some of the available positions in the CCR&R field:

GAIN Program Specialist

NOTE: This position applies to California only; check with your state's welfare department for similar programs. Under the direction of the Program Manager, the Program Specialist is responsible for providing enhanced child care resource and referral services to GAIN participants. Duties include intake, research, and delivery of referrals and guidance for choosing quality child care to GAIN participants. Specialists must also maintain statistical documentation and recordkeeping, and prepare and process reports. BA Degree in Child Development or related field required with a minimum of two years demonstrated field experience, strong written/verbal communication skills. Bilingual skills are desirable. Some knowledge of computers is needed. Salary for this position is approximately $20,000 to $25,000 per year.

Child Care Food Provider Coordinator

This person enrolls child care providers in the program and assists potential providers in becoming licensed; trains providers in nutrition and operation of the Child Care Food Program and monitors program through home visits; and coordinates social services, health, counseling, and special education referrals with providers. Qualifications needed include BA Degree and/or work experience in a child development program, ability to communicate correctly and effectively in written and oral English. The salary is $20,000 to $23,000 per year. Usually a college degree is not necessary. Apply to your state's regional offices of Food & Nutritional Services or to your local CCR&R agency.

CCR&R Counselor/Referral Specialist

This person provides child care information and referral assistance at a CCR&R agency; provides referrals to parents seeking child care via telephone, mail, and walk-in; does follow-up with parents; maintains referral files; provides written and verbal consumer information on choosing quality child care; assists with follow-up on previous referrals; participates in planning with CCR&R Coordinator or the Executive Director. Qualifications needed include BA Degree in Child Development, Early Childhood Education, Social Welfare, or related field, as well as two years work in children's programs and knowledge of child care principles and programs. (May substitute four years experience in human services or children's services for the degree.) Also needed are ability to meet the public; a pleasant telephone manner; initiative; ability to work as part of a team; skills to gather, organize, and evaluate data. Salary is 18,000 to $20,000.

CCR&R Manager

The Manager coordinates CCR&R program activities to ensure that all contract obligations are met; supervises CCR&R staff; participates in program budget planning; assists Executive Director in determining public awareness, staff in-service, legislative, and other overall operational project needs and plans to implement or adapt program to meet needs; and provides service in such areas as job bank, community resource book, new provider recruitment and visits, contract services, resource library; media and public relations; writes and edits agency newsletter; and provides technical assistance to child care providers. The Manager must have a BA Degree in ECE, Childhood Development, or Human Development; experience in providing supportive services to community; organizational skills and ability to work effectively with excessive paperwork and heavy telephone responsibilities; ability to maintain positive relationships with community, parents, providers, and staff. Salary is $25,000 to $32,000.

CCR&R Program Executive Director

The Executive Director is responsible for overall implementation and planning of CCR&R program and other funded programs; supervising CCR&R staff; developing an information and referral system and data collection system for child care consumers; arranging for and/or providing technical assistance to other agencies and child care providers; setting up training program for parents, staff, and child care providers; developing an ongoing method of needs assessment; working with staff to develop additional child care in the community; seeking funds to continue and expand project services; and submitting reports to the funding agencies. A BA or BS degree is required with two years experience in the child care field with one year in non-teaching area. Experience in administration, office procedures, fund raising, and supervision is also necessary. Salary is $32,000 to $40,000 (salaries vary from agency to agency, state to state, depending on the size of the program and the funding source).

Child Care Alternative Payment/Respite Worker

This person provides community outreach in order to recruit and enroll children in program; completes and maintains all documentation necessary for government education departments and agency auditing purposes; produces a semi-monthly child care provider payroll; and networks with other community-based agencies providing services to the client population. A BA Degree in Social Work or ECE field or equivalent experience is necessary with previous experience working in ECE or a social service agency providing services to families in distress. Also needed are ability to work independently with minimal supervision, computer literacy, and accounting aptitude. Salary expected is $18,000 to $23,000 (salaries will vary from one agency to the next, depending on the size and funding source).

A DAY IN THE LIFE OF A RESOURCE & REFERRAL AGENCY

The average CCR&R agency, with a service area of about one-half million people, receives on the average 50 to 75 incoming telephone requests each day. Also, visitors, such as parents and family day care providers, stop by, and passersby walk in off the street.

The following scenarios offer a realistic picture for some of the requests and activities that occur within a CCR&R agency.

Parent Phone Call Request

"I'm pregnant and expecting my baby next month. I'll have to return to work six weeks after the baby is born. Can you help me find good child care for my baby?"

The referral counselor spends several minutes on the phone explaining the various child care options available in her community—nannies, family day care, infant centers. The counselor explains the licensing required for family day care, the pros and cons of the various options, and the approximate costs for each type of program. Since the child care field works on supply and demand, as do other types of businesses, the counselor gives the mother-to-be a few names and asks her to call back after the baby is born for additional referrals if she so desires. The mother is encouraged to visit several referrals before making a decision. The counselor also explains about waiting lists. She usually spends about 15 to 20 minutes on the phone to explain all the various options, all the while encouraging the parent to make her own informed decision.

Job Information Request

"I'm interested in changing jobs, and I heard that you have a job bank. Right now I'm earning $5.50 an hour. Since my divorce, I'm the sole support for my two children. I need to find a better-paying position. How can I become a day care center director? I have my BA Degree."

The referral counselor interviews the woman, asking ordinary questions such as name, address, and phone number. She then questions her work experience and whether or not she has ECE college units. After obtaining these answers, the counselor discusses present job openings and how to get in touch with them. She also gives her information about the qualifications for employment at a state-funded agency, as well as how to obtain a children's center permit. The woman's name is placed on a job bank list for the next six months. In many cases, the counselor will ask for a résumé and/or schedule an interview at the office.

Employer-Related Request (Case A)

"My name is John A., and I represent the XXX Bus Company. We have 300 employees in this area, many of whom are women bus drivers in need of child care services." (During the conversation John reveals that his company came into the area by bidding low on a contract. As a consequence, the company pays the drivers a salary just above minimum wage, and to cut the company's expenses even more, they have restricted the bus drivers' schedules to split shifts and part-time hours. Child care arrangements can be difficult for these employees.)

The counselor schedules a one-hour appointment for John to discuss the various company participation options such as referrals, on-site child care, and low cost child care. After several follow-up consultations, XXX Bus Company decides to have a CCR&R counselor work with each employee on a case-to-case basis rather than offering child care benefits to their employees.

Employee-Related Request (Case B)

"My name is Gerald M., and I represent a credit union company in the south part of town. We have one of the largest facilities in the credit union field and employ more than 500 people. My supervisor asked me to check into the possibility of building a child care center on our site. We have a large open area in the back parking lot. To tell you the truth, I'm a bachelor, so I have no knowledge about kids or how to begin this project."

The CCR&R counselor sets up a one-hour appointment for Gerald M. to come into the office. At this time, the discussion will focus on surveying the needs of the employees, start-up costs for the center, an operating budget, and state and city licensing requirements. The counselor also discusses the feasibility of on-site day care as opposed to other possibilities such as vendor-voucher payments, enhanced referrals, or "cafeteria" benefits. In this case, there will likely be several follow-up calls.

Respite Care Request

A correctional officer at ZZZ Prison in San Diego calls to request that a CCR&R counselor speaks with Jim D., an inmate at the facility.

"My father-in-law was in to see you, and he says you need a letter from the prison. I guess he told you, I'm in here for at least two years. My wife has a low-paying job, so she doesn't have money to pay for child care. Right now she's leaving my baby with her cousin Shirley. I know Shirley's on drugs and sleeps most of the time. The other day my baby got hurt in Shirley's house. How can I get better child care?"

The respite counselor takes this case and speaks to the correctional officer at the prison, explaining how to write a letter to the CCR&R agency. The letter must explain that the child is in a high risk situation with the possibility of being neglected. Upon receipt of the letter, the agency can arrange for short-term child care with state funds at no cost to the parents. The respite counselor follows up on this case.

Walk-In Request

At the close of the day a young mother walks into the CCR&R office and explains her predicament. "My four kids and husband are in the car across the street and we need to go back to Arizona. Can you lend me ten dollars for gas? I just came from a church and they wouldn't loan me a quarter. I will pay you back when I get back home."

After looking at her driver's license, the counselor asks if she has food for the children. "We have milk and cookies in the car," she says.
In answer to the next question about why they're in California, the young mother replies, "A relative died and I wanted to go to the funeral. We had just enough money to get here, and nobody in the family had money to help us get back home."

With four children in the car, all appearing to be under the age of six, the office staff quickly decides to give the mother $10 from a small fund they keep in the office. This fund never includes more than $20, gathered with pennies, nickels, and dimes from the staff.

A happy mother leaves, thanking us a million times. We close the door on another busy day . . .

CCR&R RESOURCES

The National Association of Child Care Resource and Referral Agencies, with more than 200 members throughout the United States, was established in 1987 to provide a link between providers of child care and families who need child care. NACCR&RA provides leadership, stability, and support to its member agencies. Auxiliary memberships are also open to individuals and organizations supporting the goals of NACCR&RA. For more information, write or call:

NAT'L. ASSOC. OF CHILD CARE RESOURCE & REFERRAL AGENCIES
2116 Campus Dr. S.E.
Rochester, MN 55904
(507) 287-2020

The Child Care Resource and Referral Network has been functioning as a mutual support system for existing and developing CCR&R agencies in California since 1976. As a non-profit public benefit corporation, the Network represents seventy-one agencies located in fifty-seven counties throughout California.

For more information, write or call:

CALIFORNIA CHILD CARE RESOURCE AND REFERRAL NETWORK
111 New Montgomery St., 7th Floor
San Francisco, CA 94105
(415) 882-0234

8. Family Day Care

Family day care (FDC) is the perfect career for someone who loves and cares about children yet wants a home-based job. Today's concept of child care is more than just babysitting. Educated and aware parents realize the importance of good care in the child's early years. Many parents prefer a home setting for their child rather than a day care center accommodating 50 to 150 children.

A family day care home is a setting where children are cared for, usually including the mother's own preschool children. This type of home operation is especially suitable for neighborhood child care.

Although most states require six or fewer children, some states, such as California, will allow licensing for twelve children. However, the licenses for more than six children also have more government regulations — fire marshal clearance, hiring another adult worker, and conditional use permits, for example.

Before taking the necessary steps to start this business, first find out if there's a need for this service in your neighborhood, then consider the following advantages and disadvantages.

ADVANTAGES AND DISADVANTAGES

The advantages of running a family day care business include the following:

1. If you enjoy children, family day care offers the satisfaction of being with children and watching them grow and learn.
2. You can be home with your own children.
3. You'll be home when your children are sick.
4. As your own boss, you can set your own hours and vacation schedules.
5. You can choose the number and age of children you want to care for.
6. You don't have the hassle of rush hour traffic.

The disadvantages of a family day care business include:

1. The going pay rates for family day care are low in many areas.
2. Your contact all day is with children rather than adults.
3. Your home may be cluttered with cribs, playpens, etc.

4. Your own children might object to sharing their home and toys.
5. You won't have sick leave benefits, and you'll probably have to supply your own medical insurance. (Professional organizations such as NAEYC and Family Day Care Associations offer group medical insurance when you join.)

ACTIVITIES, SAFETY, AND HEALTH

Activities

Plan creative activities with the children. You will find that with planned activities, including an occasional field trip, the children seldom get bored and your hours at home doing child care are more rewarding. (Chapter 12 provides a multitude of ideas for helping children develop mentally, physically, emotionally, and intellectually.)

Safety

Before opening your family day care business, carefully consider all possibilities when it comes to the health and safety of the children. Make sure you know what to do should a disaster occur. Plan your drills in advance. Be aware that accidents and illnesses do occur, and if you plan ahead of time, you'll be able to respond calmly and effectively when problems arise.

Many states require a health and safety inspection of your home before you receive your license.

Children are naturally curious. Without any sense of danger, they will eagerly explore your home. Unfortunately, accidents are the number one threat to children. Each year approximately 14,000 children under the age of fifteen die from accidents. Toddlers, ages one to three, are most frequently poisoning victims. Never leave a child alone in your home without adult supervision.

In order to be prepared for those unexpected emergencies, take a first aid course; then keep your first aid handbook handy. Study it occasionally. In an emergency, call 911.

Here are some helpful hints for safe-proofing your home:

- Hazardous household products should be locked up or stored out of reach of crawling or climbing children.
- Keep kitchen knives, harmful cleaning products, and matches in locked cabinets.
- Put your water heater's temperature at a low setting—120 degrees F. maximum—to prevent scalding.
- Remove tablecloths that toddlers might pull off.
- Keep unused electrical outlets covered with safety caps.
- Keep all sewing items—pins, needles, scissors—out of the children's reach.

- Check your backyard and other play areas for poisonous plants.
- Flush old medicines down the drain, and keep over-the-counter drugs locked up or out of the reach of children.
- Check for peeling paint on the walls or furniture. (Lead paint is a health hazard for children.)
- Don't buy toys with small parts that can break off and be swallowed by children.

Health

Some states require family day care providers to obtain medical records from each child's physician. These records should certify that the child has no physical illness or infectious diseases, and that the necessary immunization records are up to date.

Many illnesses are not serious if proper care is given. In fact, the average child has six to nine colds a year, and they're not considered serious. Since illness is inevitable, you should establish a consistent health policy. Children who have the following symptoms should not be with other children: nausea or vomiting; diarrhea; rash, bumps, or other breaking out of the skin; pain in the ear, head, stomach, or joints; fever of 101 degrees or higher.

Keep an emergency card for each child by the telephone with the following information:

- ❏ Parent's name
- ❏ Parent's work and home phone numbers
- ❏ Names and phone numbers of friends/relatives who can pick up the child
- ❏ Physician's name and phone number
- ❏ Authorization to seek care at a local hospital
- ❏ Authorization to administer medication

AUTHORIZATION FOR EMERGENCY MEDICAL CARE

In case of accident or illness requiring immediate medical attention, the undersigned authorize _____ (day care provider) to call a physician or take our (my) child to the nearest hospital or doctor. The doctor to call is _____ (name) _____ (address) _____ (phone number), and it is understood that if possible, his/her services will be obtained. This agreement covers only those situations which, in the best judgment of the day care provider, are true emergencies. Otherwise, we (I) expect to be notified of illness or accident at once.

We (I) agree to pay all reasonable expenses incurred.
Signed:
Father _____
Mother _____
Date _____
Name of child _____

AUTHORIZATION TO ADMINISTER MEDICATION

Date: _____
I authorize the administration of _____ (medication) to _____ (child's name) by _____ (day care provider). This authorization is effective until _____ (date).
Signed:
Parent _____
Address _____
Home Phone _____ Business Phone _____

Sudden Infant Death Syndrome (SIDS)

Sometimes called "crib death," SIDS is the leading cause of death for infants one week to one year of age, with approximately two cases for every 1,000 live births. It claims the lives of seemingly healthy babies during their sleep. Yet, in spite of continuous research, scientists still do not know why these deaths occur. The death is not caused by suffocation, aspiration, or regurgitation, although these are common misconceptions.

If a SIDS death should occur, take the following steps immediately: (1) Call the emergency line 911; (2) notify the child's parents; and (3) notify your child care licensing agency.

The National SIDS Foundation and its local chapters have been formed to assist people who have experienced a SIDS death and to sponsor research into the mystery of SIDS deaths. For more information, call:

National SIDS Foundation (800) 221-7437
Greater Los Angeles Chapter (213) 663-6448

FOOD AND NUTRITION

As a family day care provider you play an important role in helping children form good attitudes about food and develop good eating habits. Nutrition experts have identified the kinds of food children should eat in order to grow and develop properly. With all the different vitamins, minerals, and other basic nutrients, nutritionists have found that it's easy to categorize foods into four basic food groups — milk, meat, vegetable/fruit, and bread/cereal.

Foods belonging in the milk group include whole milk, dry milk, cottage cheese, and pudding with milk. Young children need three or more servings from this group each day.

Foods included in the meat group can be expensive. However, some thrifty choices might be chicken, turkey, fish, ground beef, peanut butter, beans, and peas. Some vegetables such as dried beans and peas have a high protein value and are included in this group. Eggs are also included in this group. Young children need two or more servings of foods from the meat group each day.

The vegetable/fruit group is usually the easiest to plan since it includes all types of fruits and vegetables. Fresh fruits and vegetables in season are often less expensive than frozen or canned products. Young children need four or more servings a day.

Foods made from grains make up the bread/cereal group. Grains include wheat, rice, oats, and rye. Pastas, cereals, and breads are made from grains. Young children need one child-size serving of enriched cereal daily, plus bread served with each meal.

Here are some snack suggestions with selections from the four basic food groups:

Applesauce and graham cracker
Refried beans and tortilla
Cheese sticks and whole wheat crackers
Corn muffins and yogurt
Bagel and vegetable juice
Pita bread with egg salad filling
Peanut butter on crackers with milk
Grape juice and oatmeal cookies
Cheese pizza made with an English muffin

By using the four basic food groups as your guide, you can provide meals and snacks that offer a variety of nutrients. Since children are growing so rapidly, it's important for them to have good nutrition. Children who eat the right foods are happier and better able to learn.

Child Care Food Program

Because children who eat properly are happier and better able to learn, in 1968 Congress established the Child Care Program, a program of reimbursement for family day care providers. If you have one or more children in your day care home and are licensed, you are eligible for reimbursement under the program. Contact your nearest Resource & Referral agency for the address and phone number of the food program nearest to you.

Here's how the Child Care Food Program works: all meals, whether breakfast, mid-morning snack, lunch, or dinner, must meet the nutritional requirements of the United States Department of Agriculture (USDA). All children under twelve years of age may participate. Following are the 1990-91 reimbursement guidelines for each enrolled child attending your program:

Breakfast	$0.7625
Supplemental Snacks	0.41
Lunch and Dinner	1.3775

Nutrition education and menu planning assistance are available through the food program sponsor. This sponsor will visit your home approximately three times a year to verify that the children are eating well-balanced meals. You will be asked to send the sponsor your menu for the month.

DISCIPLINE

Although discipline is a part of child rearing, the word always evokes an emotional response. Essentially, the FDC provider should learn how to handle behavior problems. The goal of discipline is to set limits and to teach right from wrong.

Children under your care will all be at different stages of development and come from different backgrounds. Each child inherits characteristics and is nurtured differently in his or her cultural environment.

It's important not to be judgmental about parents. Most are trying to do their best in the job of parenting. Every child and every situation are different.

Children feel more secure if they know clearly what is acceptable behavior and what is not. The provider can let children know exactly what she means through her tone of voice, her body language, and the way she looks and touches each child. When you discipline children the right way, you are showing that you love and care about them. You want them to be happy and responsible.

Match your guidance to the child's developmental stage. Behavior that seems wrong for an older child might be normal for a younger one.

Techniques for Discipline

Time Out: When children fight, squabble, or misbehave, call "time out." Have the children involved go to a separate place for a limited period of time. Children under age five have limited memory, so three minutes for a three year old is sufficient time. This gives the child a chance to calm down and lets him know that you will not allow misbehavior in your home.

Trade Off: When children get into mischief, stop them and explain the reasons you won't allow it. Scribbling on the walls may be a problem, so make sure to provide crayons and paper for table activities or chalk boards for pictures. Organizing your home for play-learning activities prevents much of the mischief. Read stories to the children, and above all, show that you care about them.

Fix-Up: Children who cause trouble or hurt others can help in the fix-up. If a child spills milk, give her a sponge to clean it up. If one child hurts another, have him or her help with the soothing. If a youngster throws a toy, then he or she should be asked to put it away.

Corporal Punishment

Not only is corporal punishment not allowed under licensing regulations, it is morally wrong for several reasons:

- Hitting sets a bad example. It offers a poor model for handling conflict. Children learn by modeling their caregiver's behavior. If the caregiver hits them, then it's all right for them to hit others.
- Hitting is a form of violence by any name. Although you might think the word "spanking" has a better sound to it, it still means that a child is being hurt or hit by an adult.
- Hitting affects the child's self-image. Not only is the child affected, the caregiver's image is also affected. Negative discipline methods tend to stifle the child care provider's humane growth potential and creates a loss of status within the community.

When we make a commitment to treat children with respect and love, we grow into actualizing adults.

THE BUSINESS OF FAMILY DAY CARE

Always consider yourself a professional. You are offering someone's child a warm, loving home atmosphere that is safe, secure, and promotes learning through play activities. Your activities help the child developmentally, socially, and emotionally. Being professional in all aspects of your business helps you project a favorable image to parents.

Following are some of the basics for starting your own family day care business.

Setting Fees

Setting fees depends on several factors—your clients, the market rate, and the money you feel you need and deserve. You are your own boss. The prevailing market rate more or less dictates what you can charge in your area. Check with your local CCR&R agency for rates.

You'll probably have to consider the demographics about your clients. Is your home located in a blue-collar or working class neighborhood? Are both parents earning less than $25,000 combined income? Is the neighborhood composed mostly of single parents (one-wage earners)? Or do you live in an affluent neighborhood? Are there mostly two-wage earning families with combined salaries over $25,000? The answers to these questions will help determine your fees. Also, most providers charge more for taking care of infants. (Children under the age of two are usually considered infants.)

You may want to offer a lower rate for families with more than one child in your program. Many providers consider a 10 percent reduction a fair discount.

Establish with the parents when you expect to be paid. Some collect in advance, others at the end of each week or each month.

Recruiting Children

In the beginning you may need to place a newspaper advertisement. Other resources to notify about your day care service include the local CCR&R agency, local school and church offices, and local day care centers who can give your name as a referral if they are full. If possible, post business cards or flyers advertising your service in these locations.

Your phone voice and manner are important. Many parents determine whether or not they will follow through with a visit by the telephone voice.

Contracts

Most problems with the parents can be avoided if you have a clear agreement or contract. Parents should know what you expect of them. A simple contract with the parents may include the following points:

- Fee structure; when you expect payment (weekly, monthly)
- Hours of operation
- Philosophical statement on child care
- Safety-health precautions; listing of allergies or special medical problems

A meeting with the parents prior to enrollment is essential. In addition to discussing your contract, you'll need to understand the child's background—health problems, likes and dislikes, religious restrictions.

The four most important items (those causing most of the problems) to discuss with the parents are (1) money matters, (2) vacation times, (3) illnesses, and (4) discipline.

Record Keeping and Taxes

Keep accurate records of all income and expenses related to your day care business. Accurate records not only tell you how well the business is doing, but they make income tax reporting easier.

Either make or purchase a basic accounting ledger that allows you to list your income and your expenses. The "Calendar Keeper," available through Toys 'N Things Press, is an excellent method of record keeping. (See the Appendix for their address.)

Day care expenses are classified into two sections: actual (related directly to the care of children) and related (expenses for both your family and your day care children). Actual expenses include toys and equipment; food (keep these receipts separate from your family's); education and/or dues for professional organizations, subscriptions to child care journals, conferences, classes on child development; supplies, including paper, crayons, and paints. Related expenses include mortgage or rent payments; utilities (gas, electricity, water); home equipment such as washer/dryer or dishwasher; home repairs and maintenance on large appliances also used for day care business.

Refer to Schedule C on the federal and state income tax returns to determine your allowable deductions. The United States government allows family day care providers to make use of the time-space formula for related expenses.

Consult with your accountant or income tax preparer for help in setting up your records. Toys 'N Things has another excellent publication, "Basic Guide to Record Keeping and Taxes."

Income Tax Reporting

All family day care providers who receive any money for their services are required by law to file a tax report. Filing a tax report doesn't necessarily mean you'll have to pay taxes on the earnings. The initial expenses of providing family day care often offset the earnings. In fact, some providers indicate that this small business is the "last of the big writeoffs."

As a self-employed businessperson, you are required to submit a Schedule C with your tax report. You'll also have to pay into Social Security. Both forms, Schedule C and the 1040, are available at no charge from the Internal Revenue Service.

9. Child Care Center

Certainly one of the dreams for many child care teachers and center directors is to own and operate their own child care centers. Not only does this business offer a sense of satisfaction in watching children grow and develop, it also promises an attractive profit in today's offerings of child care opportunities.

Once you make the decision to open your own center, you will be placing yourself in the position of a small business owner—a child care entrepreneur. Success comes to the small business owner who makes an investment of time, money, and energy.

RESPONSIBILITIES INVOLVED

Before you embark on the idea of opening a child care center, let's look at some of the responsibilities. Do you have an understanding of what is needed to provide quality child care successfully?

To meet licensing requirements in most states, you will need a certain number of child development course units as well as experience in working with children. And, to be most successful, you'll likely want to be both owner and director.

In addition to recognizing the business details associated with being an entrepreneur, you will need a clear understanding of the responsibilities that go with being a child care center director. Here are some of the tasks:

- Interacting with both parents and children.
- Recruiting and hiring staff.
- Keeping the staff apprised of professional and legislative activities.
- Finding substitute teachers as backups.
- Helping the teachers plan their programs.
- Planning staff meetings and preparing a staff handbook.
- Showing prospective parents and students around the center.
- Arranging conferences with parents.
- Overseeing the facility, equipment, food, and supplies.
- Maintaining adequate health and safety programs.
- Working with other child care professionals in the community.

A Word About Regulations

In order to protect the safety and well-being of children, most states have established regulations for opening a child care center.

Your first step will be to get in touch with your state's child care regulatory office. In some states this may be Social Services and in others, Health and Human Services. These agencies will provide copies of the state regulations, outlining the procedures you should follow to obtain licensing.

Generally speaking, licensing regulations cover such areas as physical space (the number of indoor and outdoor square feet needed per child), health requirements, staff/child ratios, food preparation and nutrition, emergency procedures, educational program requirements, discipline, and recordkeeping.

Then you must check with your city's zoning department and find out what areas are zoned for child care centers.

Contact your county's Building Department and check into building code requirements. You will need an occupancy permit from this department before you can open your business. Talk to your local fire marshal about the fire codes in your community.

Check with your state's Health Department for regulations on such things as plumbing, food preparation, equipment, and ventilation.

Choose a name for your center and apply for a Fictitious Business name.

Although most people operate their child care centers as sole proprietors, you may want to seek legal advice about other types of business arrangements such as partnerships or subcontracting to employer groups.

Protect your center with insurance coverage. Policies differ from state to state, so discuss the different types of coverage with your local agent. Liability and accident insurance are considered essential.

SELECTING YOUR LOCATION

Selecting a location for your child care center may be one of your most important decisions, not only in terms of attracting business, but also in determining your start-up expenses.

Before making any decisions on location, establish that there's a need for child care services in the area. Take a look at your competition and find out what they're offering. The ideal location, of course, would be found in a high need area with few competing child care centers.

Several factors to consider when selecting your location include:

- Visibility to passing drivers
- Meets licensing requirements
- Zoned for a child care center

- Accessibility for parents
- Proximity to elementary schools
- Crime-free, safe area
- Sufficient outdoor and indoor space
- Adequate kitchen and bathroom facilities

In seeking the ideal location, you may want to explore several different resources—homes or condominiums listed in the classified real estate ads; local churches or synagogues; property management companies; and commercial contractors.

Today, many child care center operators are opening facilities in suburban shopping centers that have access to outside areas. Check at your local shopping malls or contact developers or commercial brokers in your community. Take your time and negotiate such items as outside space, fencing for the children's playground, bathroom facilities, carpeting, windows, and room divisions.

If you have any doubts about the location you are contemplating, give your state's licensing specialist a call. In many states these specialists will inspect the proposed facility and give you a cost estimate for making the facility meet the licensing requirements.

BUILDING CRITERIA

The size of your facility will determine the size of your program. State licensing regulations specify exactly how many square feet are necessary per child, both indoors and outdoors. For example, in California the state mandates 35 square feet of indoor space for each preschool or school-age child, and for infants additional square footage is required to accommodate cribs. California's centers must also allot 75 square feet of usable outdoors space, excluding the swimming pool area.

Child care center classrooms should be bright, cheerful, and well ventilated. Several small classrooms with small groups give children greater experiences than large classrooms with all ages of children.

Durable classrooms that can handle spilled materials, scribbles, and inevitable fingerprints are designed with fire-resistant and easy-to-clean materials. Carpet some of the floor space since children spend much of their time playing or sitting on the floor.

Plumbing requirements for child care centers are usually more extensive than for other types of businesses. Your licensing agency will specify the number of toilets necessary and whether or not you'll need separate bathrooms for boys and girls.

Storage is another important factor in planning your building design. Plan for a central storage area as well as closets and cupboard space in the individual classrooms. You may want to consider an outdoor storage shed for playground equipment.

An office and staff lounge will give both you and your staff some privacy during the day.

MAKING PLANS

In one respect, opening a child care center is no different than opening any other type of business — any business will fail without good, steady business management. To improve your chances for success, you will want to be knowledgeable in several areas of running a business — bookkeeping, taxes, management skills, budgeting, and marketing.

You may want to take some basic business classes before opening your center. If your budget permits, hired consultants can help you get started. Other sources of business help include SCORE (Service Core of Retired Executives) and the Small Business Administration.

By all means, develop a business plan. In fact, if you're seeking financial assistance, it will be essential to have one. Not only will your business plan help you develop as a business manager, it gives you a path to follow. The time you invest now in developing a written business plan will pay off once your business is opened.

Each business plan reflects its own unique characteristics, style, and philosophy. Your business plan should run from 6 to 20 pages. The following outline indicates some of the areas you will want to cover.

TITLE PAGE
  Company Name/Address/Phone Number
  Preparation Date
EXECUTIVE SUMMARY
  Usually written last, this summary is a concise explanation of your company's current status in relation to the services provided at your center; the unique features of your child care center; your financial projections; and your long-term goals (3 to 5 years).
TABLE OF CONTENTS
BUSINESS HISTORY
  Founding date; the center's legal structure; a description of your business; and your goals for the center.
SERVICES
  Description of your services, including hours of operation, ages of children you will serve, if transportation will be provided for school-age children, and if lunches will be served.
MARKET ANALYSIS
  Analyze your prospective parents' expectations and write up a customer profile; discuss the current trends in the child care field and how you intend to capitalize on these trends; identify your competitors and their share of the child care market, their weaknesses, their strengths,

and how your services will differ; explain how your rates compare with your competitors' rates. (To find out what the local market rates are, contact your local CCR&R agency, or call some local child care centers and ask what their weekly or monthly rates are for the different age groups.)

MARKET STRATEGY

Develop an advertising (promotional) strategy; list your advertising techniques.

FACILITY

Explain the nature of your center and outdoor play space; amount of square footage; play equipment and learning materials; accessibility of your location to your prospective customers. (Today's parents are searching for facilities that keep their child safe, secure, and happy.)

MANAGEMENT/STAFF

Identify the key individuals in running your child care center; summarize their history; describe their specific duties and contributions to your overall goals; discuss compensation and salary levels.

FINANCIAL STATEMENTS AND PROJECTIONS

Include the financial forms listed on the following pages of this chapter.

FINANCIAL CONSIDERATIONS

Essentially, there are four ways to finance a new business—your own money, investors, institutional sources (banks, S&Ls, credit unions), and the Small Business Administration. To obtain financing from a bank or other financial institution, you will probably have to cover approximately 30 percent of the projected expenses out of your pocket.

Many state licensing regulatory agencies require you to have three months of operating funds before they will issue your license. These agencies want to make certain that you can meet your payroll and lease payments or mortgage obligations even if you are not up to full capacity after opening. Remember that parental fees are your only source of income.

When planning your program, take into consideration that most mothers who go back to work need care for children under two years of age. Not only do these infants and toddlers need tender loving care, you will need more staff to meet these children's needs. In fact, many states require a 1:4 staff/child ratio for infants and a 1:6 staff/child ratio for toddlers. You can ask a higher fee for children who are not toilet trained.

In a recent survey across the country, the market rates for infant care in the large metropolitan areas ranged from $100/week to $140/week. Toddler fees averaged $85 to $100 per week. Rates for preschool children were in the $70 to $80 range.

Child care is a highly labor-intensive industry, so the greatest percentage of your budget, approximately 55-75 percent, will go for salaries.

Start-Up Budget

The start-up expenses you incur are dependent on several variables. These variables include whether or not you will be building a new facility or renting or leasing an existing building, the size of your child care center, and the proposed number of children. The following form will help you determine your particular start-up budget:

INCOME AMOUNT

Bank loan _____
Gifts and contributions _____
Other _____
Subtotal _____

EXPENSES AMOUNT

FACILITY
Down payment or purchase of facility _____
Remodeling/renovation expenses _____
Rent/lease deposits _____
Utility deposits _____

PERSONNEL
(expenses prior to opening, see note) _____

EQUIPMENT
Inside furniture such as cabinets,
   tables, chairs, and napping cots _____
Inside play equipment such as puzzles,
   blocks, and books _____
Outside play equipment _____
Office equipment _____

SUPPLIES
Arts and crafts supplies _____
Housekeeping (toilet paper, cleaning, etc.) _____
Office/business supplies _____
Food supplies _____

LEGAL AND PROFESSIONAL FEES
Licensing expenses _____
Attorney's fees _____
Consultant fees _____

MISCELLANEOUS
Advertising expenses _____
Insurance _____
Subtotal _____

Note: Many state regulating agencies will not allow an owner to be the director of a day care center if he or she does not have an ECE education or experience. In such cases, you will incur the expense of a part-time salary for a director whose help you will need in getting the center open.

Annual Operating Budget

You will need to establish an operating budget, making sure you have enough money to cover expenses for the first 60 to 90 days. Following is a sample operating budget to help you project your annual expenses:

INCOME

Fees	Per Child Per Year	Number of Children	Totals
Infant	_____	X _____	_____
18 to 30 mo.	_____	X _____	_____
2½ to 5 yrs.	_____	X _____	_____
Total Income			_____

EXPENSES

Salaries	_____
Payroll Taxes	_____
Staff Training	_____
Mortgage Payment/Lease	_____
Insurance	_____
Utilities	_____
Advertising	_____
Accounting & Bookkeeping	_____
Office Supplies	_____
Food	_____
Art & Educational Matls.	_____
Furniture & Equipment	_____
Field Trips	_____
Janitorial	_____
Repairs & Maintenance	_____
Other	_____
Total Expenses	_____

EQUIPMENT AND MATERIALS

In addition to planning a center that meets all the licensing requirements, take plenty of time in selecting appropriate equipment and learning materials. You may want to use the services of a consultant in planning your services. For more information on start-up materials, equipment, and design, contact Kaplan School Supply Corp., 1310 Lewisville-Clemmons Road, Lewisville, NC 27023 (800) 334-2014.

Outdoor Playground

The outdoor play area should be both fun and safe. You will be required to have a sturdy fence, usually five feet high to meet licensing regulations, with good latches.

Make sure the outdoor equipment you select is safe as well as attractive. Outdoor equipment is subject to constant heavy usage, so don't cut any corners here.

Indoor Equipment and Materials

Again, you may want to involve a consultant or your staff in the selection of equipment and supplies. Special "interest" areas in your classrooms will help enrich the lives of the youngsters. These specialized areas, each demanding special supplies and materials, may include music, language, art, blocks, manipulative devices, science, housekeeping, dress-up, and motor skills development.

SELECTING AND WORKING WITH YOUR STAFF

When all is said and done, your staff serves as a reflection of your program philosophy and goals. These are the people who help build your good reputation. Make certain you have a well-defined idea of the type of person you are looking for, check his or her references carefully, and follow up on his or her interaction with the children.

Your state's licensing agency will establish the minimum guidelines for the number of staff you'll need in relation to the number of children. Staff/child ratios vary from state to state, but generally they run in the 1:8 to 1:12 range for preschool-age children.

As you begin looking for qualified staff, consider contacting the following places: local CCR&R agency, college placement offices, state licensing office, employment agencies, vocational high schools, and networking organizations such as NAEYC.

To work with your staff in the most efficient manner possible, spend time in developing your programs and policies.

- Develop a staff schedule.
- Write up job description contracts for all staff members including yourself.
- Establish a competitive wage level and consider possible fringe benefits such as health insurance, vacation time, sick leave, maternity leave, retirement plan, paid staff training for workshops, additional college credits, and conferences.
- Write a personnel policy so your employees know what to expect and include salary ranges, benefits, hiring and termination policies, evaluation procedures, grievance procedure, and sick and vacation time.

DEVELOPING YOUR PROGRAM

The true essence of your child care service is your daily program—everything children experience during the day. Several resources are available in planning your curriculum. Many of the organizations listed in the Appendix can be an invaluable guide in developing your program.

Your choices in curriculum will be dictated by the developmental levels of the children in your center. Keep in mind, however, that children need both structured and unstructured time for learning and experimenting activities. (Check Section II in this book for curriculum ideas.)

Your biggest responsibility will be to encourage the children and to give them a sense of self-respect and accomplishment. As the owner of a day care center, you will be providing the opportunities and materials they need to develop in the ways they choose.

PROMOTING YOUR CHILD CARE CENTER

Promoting or marketing your business involves communicating with your prospective customers to produce favorable action. Promotion can be as simple as handing out a business card or as elaborate as staging a celebrity-studded event. In other words, promoting your child care center can be as extensive as you care to make it.

Establishing an effective marketing program, an important element in your business plan, can be the key to your success. Consider your promotion efforts as an investment in your business.

Most small business owners have learned that it takes money to make money. As the owner, you will have to make the final decisions on how best to promote your business. All in all, keep your promotional efforts simple, manageable, and affordable. Following are some suggestions, many quite inexpensive:

Resource and Referral Agency

At no charge to you, your local CCR&R agency will work with you in building up your child care business. Contact the National Association for Child Care Resource and Referral Agencies for an agency in your area. (See Chapter 7 for the address.)

Press Release

At the cost of a postage stamp, the press release mailed to your community paper may be one of the least expensive methods of announcing the opening of your center. Press releases are run at the paper's discretion on a space available basis. In writing the press release, stick to the facts only. This isn't the time to add glowing adjectives about your prospective center. You may want to make a follow-up phone call, asking the newspaper staff about the status of your press release.

Flyers

Another inexpensive way to advertise your center is to distribute flyers in such public places as shopping centers and community centers. Post your flyer in laundromats and restaurants.

Business Cards

Business cards can be both inexpensive and effective. Have the cards printed with the center's name, your name, address, phone number, business hours, and the ages of children you want to care for. Ask your friends and relatives to hand out your business cards. Take a few cards to nearby elementary schools for the office staff to have on hand. (Ask if they will hand out your flyers, too.)

Newspaper Advertising

Newspaper advertising may be handled in two ways — classified and display. Classified ads in the appropriate section of your local newspaper are inexpensive, yet they're usually well read. To be effective, display advertising requires a strong headline, good body copy, and usually a visual/photo of some type. As part of their service, your local newspaper can help you with a display ad.

Yellow Pages

Many prospective parents look in the Yellow Pages for nearby child care centers. People using the Yellow Pages are ready to take action, so include as much information as possible. Make certain your phone number is in large print.

Brochures

Nicely designed brochures can serve as effective handouts, especially at libraries, women's groups, colleges, universities, churches, PTAs, and personnel agencies. You may want to seek help for the design of your brochure from a graphic artist, printer, or advertising agency.

Word-of-Mouth

Dollar for dollar, you can't beat word-of-mouth advertising. Although this type of advertising takes longer, it's one of the best.

Networking

Wherever and whenever possible, discuss your child care center. Make announcements at group meetings. Join local and national child care organizations. These are all wonderful opportunities to discuss your center and make contact with prospective employees and customers.

THE NEED FOR QUALITY CARE

Today's parents are more informed, and rightly so, about child care facilities and how to choose quality care for their children. They want the center that will be of greatest benefit to their child's well-being.

Parents may want a parent-provider agreement so they can know what to expect from your services and what their responsibilities will be.

You can expect prospective parents to visit your facility, among others, to find the quality of care they want for their children. Here's what "quality" child care provides:

Safety and Security:
Are toys and equipment clean and unbroken?
Are outdoor fencing and latches adequate?
Is the drop-off/pick-up area safe?

Comfort:
Does the center have controlled temperature?
Are the lunches and snacks nutritious?
Are drinking fountains available?

Staff:
Does the staff have appropriate child development backgrounds and training?
Have most of the staff been in the program for at least one year?
Are the staff/child ratios appropriate for the age groups?
Are staff members responsive and supportive?

Guidance/Discipline:
What methods of discipline are used?
How is a child's anger handled?
Is guidance matched to each child's age?
Are the rules clearly stated?
Is there a consistency in the enforcement of rules?

Growth Opportunities:
Is there enough space for active and quiet play?
Are the pieces of equipment and supplies age-appropriate?
Is there an ample supply and a variety of toys?
Does the center have climbing equipment?
Does the center offer field trips?

Love and Respect:

Are the children treated with kindness?

Does the center strive to show caring concern and interest in the children?

Do the teachers avoid favoritism?

Do the teachers listen to the children?

Above all, provide warm, loving care for the children who attend your center and you'll soon find a waiting list of parents who know that your center will keep their child safe, secure, and happy.

10. New Century Careers

Today, as society comes under greater pressures and risks, career seekers have the unusual opportunity of extending their horizons to meet these challenges. If you choose to seek these new horizons in child care, rest assured that you will take your conscience to work every day.

Social policies in America are often contradictory, mainly because they are affected by ethnographic changes and political pressures. Child development researchers tell us that the first few years of a person's life play a crucial role in shaping lifelong mental, emotional, and physical abilities. Yet as our society moves into the new century, the social investments we make regarding the early years in children's lives are made grudgingly.

The following statistics illustrate the mounting crisis of our children and repudiate everything America professes to be:

- Approximately one in five children lives in poverty.
- Child abuse and neglect have grown to more than two million cases each year with about 900,000 verified.
- Statistics show an increased rate of children born with disabilities including developmental, sensory, orthopedic, and retardation. The exact number of children with these conditions is difficult to measure. However, as an example, some 106,092 children received special education services in Los Angeles County in 1986.
- In some inner-city hospitals more than one in ten babies are born drug-exposed.
- Some 3.3 million children are now living with their teenage mothers; the proportion of out-of-wedlock births to teenagers has soared during the past 20 years.

Because these alarming conditions prevail, it is easy to generate sympathy for these children who suffer through no fault of their own. We as citizens, and job seekers, may want to become involved in changing these deplorable conditions. Some of the areas you might consider exploring include educating the public, empowering citizens, changing institutional behaviors, and best of all — taking your consciousness into the workplace by starting your career with special needs children.

Some of the job opportunities for taking your consciousness into the workplace in child care include: Child Protection Social Worker; Child Development Specialist for Drug-Exposed Babies; Disabled Children Personnel (Advocates, Occupational Therapists, Speech and Language Therapists); intergenerational workers; and child care lobbyists.

CHILD PROTECTION SOCIAL WORKER (CPSW)

If you are people-oriented and interested in working with both children and adults, a position as a child protection social worker, although stressful, can be exceptionally rewarding. Social workers specializing in child protection services are dedicated, hard-working professionals who meet with families and children to identify the problems creating child abuse and neglect. Using a case management approach, these workers provide a variety of support services to families of these children.

Types of Family Support Services

Emergency Response: As a child service worker, you investigate and follow up on reported incidents of suspected child abuse, neglect, or abandonment. In Los Angeles approximately 5,000 calls are made to the Child Abuse Hotline each month. Once the telephone screener determines the geographic area where the alleged abuse has occurred, a team of social workers responds within a two-hour period.

You will conduct face-to-face interviews with children and parents and arrange for emergency placement of the children in shelter care facilities. Additionally, you will provide counseling and other support to the family.

Family Maintenance: The CPSW provides protective services to children in their homes, provided they can remain home safely. This service emphasizes correcting home conditions that lead to abuse. You may need to refer the child and parents to community agencies for therapy, parent training, and other support services. Nowadays, many of these children are referred to day care centers where they can grow and develop in a nurturing environment that stimulates intellectual and emotional growth. During the evening and weekend hours, the child is reunited with his parents. Parents may be asked to attend counseling sessions or parent training classes (see Chapter 5 on "Respite Worker's Duties").

Family Reunification: If a child is removed from his or her home, the CPSW focuses on reuniting the family and at the same time correcting the conditions that cause the abuse. As a CPSW, you will set up and supervise visitation between children and their families. While monitoring the child's well-being, it sometimes becomes necessary to remove the child and place him in a more appropriate home.

Emergency Planning: When the Social Services Department and Juvenile Court determine that a child cannot be reunited with his or her family or when reunification has failed, your duty will be to locate a permanent alternative home, a home that offers a stable and nurturing environment. These alternatives include adoption, guardianship, and long-term foster care. During this planning period, you will also make referrals for medical and psychological assessment of the child.

Qualifications for the Child Protective Social Worker

Similar to other governmental positions, there are different entry-level positions for the CPSW. The majority of workers are employed by county and state government agencies such as the Department of Social Services.

Children's Social Worker Trainee: This is usually the title for the first entry level position. To qualify for this position you will need a bachelor's degree from an accredited college with a major in psychology, sociology, social work, child development, or a related human services field.

Children Social Worker I: For this position you will need one year's experience as a Children's Social Worker Trainee or a BA degree from an accredited college with one of the same majors listed for the trainee and one year of paid experience in a social service agency providing protective placement casework services to children and families. The salary schedule is adjusted to your experience and/or college degree.

Children Social Worker II: This position requires a Master's degree in social work, marriage and family counseling, or psychological counseling or a BA in psychology, sociology, social welfare, child development, or related human services field and two years of social work experience. Your experience may include rendering social services to wards or dependent children of the court during the preceding five years.

CPSW Job Sites and Salaries

Apply to your nearest Department of Social Services, listed in the telephone directory under "Government Agencies." This position is considered one of the fastest growing opportunities during the next decade.

The average monthly salary for CPSWs in large metropolitan areas such as New York or Los Angeles runs approximately $2,200 per month in the entry level positions. This salary includes such fringe benefits as deferred compensation plans and medical insurance.

In 1991 starting salaries for those holding Master's degrees averaged approximately $2,850 per month.

Professional Organizations

The following two organizations provide additional information about child protection social work:

NATIONAL ASSOCIATION OF SOCIAL WORKERS
7981 Eastern Ave.
Silver Spring, MD 20910

COUNCIL SOCIAL WORK EDUCATION
111 Eighth Ave.
New York, NY 10011

WORKERS FOR SPECIAL NEEDS CHILDREN AND CHILDREN WITH DISABILITIES

The U.S. population of children with disabilities has been growing dramatically over the past few years. Today, some 10 percent of all children are born mentally retarded, hard of hearing, speech impaired, cerebral palsy, orthopedically impaired, or otherwise impaired.

As we approach the 21st century, many new job opportunities will be opening for people interested in meeting the needs of these special children and their families. In these positions you will play a role in the social changes our country is presently undergoing. Once you open your heart and mind to becoming a mover and shaker, you will touch these children's lives as you help them become "the best they can be."

If you choose to work as an advocate of this special population of children, you will need to understand the background of our public laws and how they have affected services to these children. Following is a chronology of important events in the establishment of the standards we know today:

1864—President Lincoln signed a bill creating Gallaudet College, an institution of higher education for the deaf.

1869—Boston, MA established the first public school for the deaf.

1890—Providence, RI established classes for the mentally retarded at public schools.

1911—New Jersey became the first state to adopt a special education law.

1966—Congress created a grant program for the states to educate children with disabilities. The federal government created a Bureau of Education for the Handicapped (BEH), now called the Office of Special Education within the Department of Education.

1970 — Congress enacted Public Law 91-230, the Education of the Handicapped Act (EHA). This act authorized funding for regional centers for deaf and blind children and experimental early childhood programs.

1975—A national deadline of 1980 was established, requiring states to educate children with disabilities. This was called part B of EHA (commonly known as Public Law 94-142). This law guarantees each child, ages three and older, a free and appropriate education.

Public Law 99-457

In 1986 Congress enacted Public Law 99-457 to assist families who have disabled children from birth to three years of age. Families may receive early intervention services for their children, ages birth to three years. This act awards grants to states for the development and expansion of comprehensive services for disabled infants and toddlers and their families.

Following are highlights of this law. States are required to:

- Adopt a definition of developmentally disabled.
- Develop a timetable to provide services within five years.
- Compile a central directory of services and experts.
- Establish a comprehensive child find and referral system.
- Use Individual Family Service Plans, including case management.
- Establish a contracting process or make other arrangements with service providers.
- Develop a payment system.
- Conduct a public awareness program.

With the passage of this law, careers in the field of disabled children are enjoying renewed interest.

PEDIATRIC REHABILITATION SERVICES

Sarah Keeny: A "Mover and Shaker"

Sarah Keeny, Center Director, Children's Services Center at the world-renowned Casa Colina, is an example of one of today's wonderful advocates for the rights of all children. Sarah believes that all children are entitled to grow, to experience their world, and to become the very best they can be.

Sarah and the staff at Casa Colina value every individual regardless of age. From birth to adolescence, they recognize the special rehabilitation needs of these children. While adults have occupations and roles in society, children have their own jobs to do—to grow up learning about the world, themselves, and others.

Sarah believes that the family is important to a child's successful growth and learning, so Casa Colina's pediatric services are family centered.

Positions in the Pediatric Rehabilitation Field

Casa Colina and other rehabilitation facilities across the nation can provide rewarding and satisfying long-term careers. Pediatric rehabilitation provides services to children with neurological, orthopedic, and other medical needs. These multi-disciplinary, in-patient and out-patient services include special programs for infant development (mild head injuries); learning disabilities including attention deficit and hyperactivity (ADHD); coma regulation; and swallowing disorders.

For more information contact:
CHILDREN'S SERVICES CENTER
Casa Colina
255 E. Bonita Ave.
Pomona, CA 91767
(714) 593-7521

A variety of positions is available for people interested in working with special needs children. These professional positions, which do require college degrees, include: physicians, speech and language specialists, physical therapists, occupational therapists, recreational therapists, nurses, psychologists, social workers, and child development specialists.

However, Sarah is presently advocating that many of these services be provided by semi-skilled people who receive on-the-job training. If this work interests you, check with several rehabilitation facilities and explain your interest. You may well become one of the first trainees in this exciting and growing field.

CHILD CARE JOB OPPORTUNITIES IN A DRUG-ABUSED WORLD

While most of us will agree that "to be born healthy is the right of every child," many of today's drug-exposed children aren't enjoying this right. Martin Luther King Hospital, Los Angeles, reports that some 100 drug-exposed babies are born each month.

At Prentice Women's Hospital of Northwestern Memorial Hospital, Chicago, 1982 studies indicated that three percent of their patients had been using sedative or hypnotic drugs (marijuana, benzodiazepines, tranquilizers, or alcohol). This figure has likely increased every subsequent year and will likely continue doing so in the years to come.

Cocaine is considered one of today's popular glamour drugs. Yet, studies show that it's more dangerous to an unborn child than any other illicit drug.

Because drug-exposed babies usually have lower birth weights, are shorter, and have smaller head circumferences than infants delivered to drug-free mothers, they are frequently irritable and withdrawn. These mothers (feeling guilt and worry over their drug use) have difficult times responding to and interacting with their babies. The bonding process is hindered, so child abuse and neglect increases among infants born to mothers using drugs.

With this gloomy information coming into the forefront, is it any wonder that governmental, private, and religious programs have begun to flourish to help these mothers and to give these babies a chance? These babies are the future of our society.

Working with Drug-Exposed Children

Although the concept of providing help for drug-exposed babies is somewhat new to our society, several programs have already been established and more will develop in the upcoming years. One of the newer programs is being developed through Head Start.

Recently, through a grant awarded by the Department of Health and Human Services, Head Start began a three-year pilot program for medically fragile infants at Charles Drew University, Compton, CA. In an effort to address the escalating problem of drug-exposed children, this new program has developed a state-of-the-art, community-based child care center as well as home-based programs for children ages birth to three years.

According to Program Coordinator Hanna Hunter-Hamilton, the Project Head Start program offers each child an opportunity to learn and grow at his own pace in a stimulating preschool educational environment or home setting at no cost to the parents. Family service plans are developed for each individual child and his parents. Children receive a complete physical and dental examination as well as daily breakfasts, hot lunches, and snacks.

Children ages birth to eighteen months participate in the home-based program. They are assigned a family service worker, one of today's new career positions. This person provides a variety of services to the families twice a week in their homes. If this position interests you and you have a child development background, check with your local Head Start program for this or similar positions.

Children eighteen months to three years of age participate in the center-based program. These children attend preschool four hours daily, five days a week. The centers, set up in accordance with the High/Scope® curriculum, provide a stimulating education environment. Most preschool teachers and directors will qualify for positions in these centers.

In addition to the center-based and home-based programs, Project Head Start also works with parents, making them aware of the following services: child treatment/child diagnosis; child prognosis and community resources; child rights; developmental/disability laws and regulations (parents are taught how to communicate with physicians and other medical personnel).

Since many drug-exposed children are not living with their biological mothers, social workers make plans for reunification. They support both the biological mother and the foster parent. Support groups are provided to help substance abusing parents become drug free. Other groups help reduce isolation, thereby decreasing the risk for potential child abuse.

For more information contact:

CHARLES R. DREW UNIVERSITY OF MEDICINE AND SCIENCE
Project Head Start
1314 E. Compton Blvd.
Compton, CA 90221
(213) 605-1506

Aspiring child development specialists who are interested in helping these unfortunate babies and toddlers will find new positions as more and more programs are developed to help drug-exposed children.

INTERGENERATIONAL PROGRAMS

Dora Keyser Stoller (1899-1984), a woman who dedicated her life to humanitarian pursuits, was someone who truly cared. Not only did she care about people, young and old, she put action into her words.

Because she believed in freedom and justice for all people, Dora spent untold hours making and selling ceramic items to raise funds for worthy causes. In fact, Caesar Chavez of the United Farm Worker's Union made a special trip to meet the "lovely lady" who had raised more than $50,000 for his organization.

Throughout her life, working with young children was one of her treasured pursuits. She not only loved and respected youngsters, she understood how they learned about the world. Frederick Froebel, Maria Montessori, and John Dewey were part of her life. She understood progressive education and practiced it.

Dora was a strong advocate for volunteerism in the Head Start program; how delightfully she described the joys of working and playing with four year olds. Many of the little ones in her life were recipients of her specially made felt-covered balls and hand-designed blocks.

Truly an example of the intergenerational spirit, this section on intergenerational programs is dedicated to Dora Keyser Stoller.

The Background of Intergenerational Programs

Intergenerational programs encourage interaction between the generations to replace stereotyped perceptions with healthy attitudes. American society is an age-segregated culture compared to other countries around the world. From preschool to high school, young people attend schools where they are placed in classes according to age rather than development. The middle-aged generation, ages 30 to 60, make up our work force. And our older citizens pursue activities with their own age group, with many of the activities in senior citizen centers where these seniors are segregated from other age groups.

According to Margaret Mead, we need to understand the past in order to make decisions about the present and the future. As programs have developed that link the old and the young in educational services, they do more than bridge the gap. These programs encourage a sense of responsibility among the young about the future of our society.

Many successful intergenerational programs have sprung from retirement homes and nursing facilities. When the old and the young share listening, gardening, music, storytelling, and crafts, this mutual sharing of activities and ideas results in feelings of self-worth for both generations.

The 1990 census tells us that older adults make up the fastest growing portion of our population. By the year 2000, older adults will number 20 percent of the population.

Numerous job positions in child care centers and preschools, or as a family day care provider, are open to adults between the ages of 55 and 75. Many of these older adults find themselves reentering the job market, some for the first time and others because of layoffs or early retirements.

How Lee F. Has Prepared for Retirement

Sixty-two year old Lee F. is one example of someone fulfilling an intergenerational role. Lee, who plans to retire next year, has worked all her life in office positions such as banking and bookkeeping. A highly energetic person, Lee wanted a new, rewarding challenge in her life after retirement.

"Young children give me the greatest joy when they laugh and play," she says. Not having any grandchildren herself, Lee has volunteered her spare time in a day care center near her home. She is now enrolled in a college class on Child Growth and Development in preparation for her new career.

Finding a position in a day care center will be easy for Lee. She is a willing, productive worker who cares about the well-being of children and their families. Also, this new job will help supplement her Social Security pension.

Elvirita Lewis Center

Many day care center operators consider older adults, even those without schooling or training, as "naturals" when it comes to staffing their centers. The Foundation for the Elvirita Lewis Center, Santa Cruz, California, became the pioneer of intergenerational programs in 1975.

They first developed a corps of substitute teachers (always in high demand), each of whom is scheduled to work one day a week. These older substitute workers receive on-site experience in working with young children, so eventually they become part of the intake process for those seeking employment at the center. The Foundation has found that although these older workers might be slower than the younger staff, they make fewer errors, and they use sound judgment.

According to Steven Brummel, President, Foundation for the Elvirita Lewis Center, the University of Nevada in Reno, has planned a new program for older adults who are reentering the workforce. This exciting and innovative program offers older adults training with young children in a family day care setting. Using an extensive training model, older adults are taught how to start their own home-based child care businesses or how to work in another person's home. The program also helps with Start-Up expenses and equipment costs.

When older adults finish their training program, Brummel predicts that their income will be around $20,000 a year. He also foresees similar programs being offered at other colleges and universities using the University of Nevada model.

Author's Note: As the teacher of a Family Day Care training course at a local community college for six years, I've found that approximately 30 percent of my students are over the fifty-year mark. Now with Federal Grant Block monies being allocated to the states with an emphasis on training child care providers, we can anticipate seeing new programs and new careers emerging.

Broome County Intergenerational Program

Another interesting intergenerational activities program was begun in 1980 in Broome County, New York. The emphasis of this program is to encourage young children's visits to retirement homes and older adults' visits to early childhood program sites. With careful planning and ongoing coordination between program leaders, this program continues to meet with success. The Broome County program has twelve early childhood programs exchanging regular visits with thirteen geriatric facilities.

If you enjoy working with both age groups, you may find the position of coordinator in this type of program both challenging and rewarding. As coordinator you will work with various community groups and report to a Child Care Council. Your duties will include arranging transportation, providing support, and developing meaningful and successful intergenerational experiences.

Foster Grandparent Program (FGP)

Although the Foster Grandparent Program (FGP) was instituted in 1965, few people seem to be aware of this program. Additionally, little material about the program is available. Administered by the federal government's Action Agency, FGP was established to benefit children with special needs and low-income aging people who crave meaningful activity and personal relationships. To qualify for employment, Foster Grandparents must be over sixty years of age and meet the federal guidelines of low income. No educational requirements need to be met. However, program participants must be in good health with no physical handicaps. Women who have never worked outside the home before as well as farmers, teachers, nurses, and clerks are some of the people who have been accepted into the program.

If you are in a lower income bracket and over sixty years of age, the Foster Grandparent Program may give you a chance at employment while offering an opportunity to help deserving youngsters with special needs. Before beginning employment, you will receive forty hours of orientation training and four hours a month of in-service training.

Once you have completed training, you may choose a nearby facility for employment. Your choices include handicapped developmental disabilities facilities, youth houses, Head Start programs, and correctional facilities. You will be employed for twenty hours per week and divide your time among two or three children. You will receive a nontaxable hourly stipend, a daily meal, vacation time, and insurance.

Mary L., age seventy, is one jovial Foster Grandparent who works at a juvenile facility. "I look forward to being with my 'Boys' on a regular basis. I feel like a real grandmother to them," says Mary. Not lucky enough to have her own grandchildren, she takes delight in telling her friends about her special "grandsons."

When grandson Dean raised the flag for the opening ceremonies of a special event at the facility, Mary's face beamed with joy as he accomplished his feat. Her love for him and his respect for her have made a remarkable change in Dean's life. A child whose life was fraught with the misery of child abuse now has a grandmother who cares about him. When Dean enters the rehabilitation process he will always remember Mary, his special grandma.

Resources for Intergenerational Programs

RETIRED SENIOR VOLUNTEER PROGRAMS ACTION AGENCY
Foster Grandparents
Public Affairs Office
1100 Vermont Ave. NW
Washington, DC 20525
(202) 634-9108

(Each state has an ACTION Office. Check the white pages of your telephone book for the address and phone number.)

THE ELVIRITA LEWIS FOUNDATION
P.O. Box 1539
La Quinta, CA 92253
(619) 564-1780
President: Steven W. Brummel

BROOME COUNTY INTERGENERATIONAL ACTIVITIES PROGRAM
Broome County Developmental Council
29 Fayette St.
Birmingham, NY 13901
(607) 723-8313

CHILD CARE AND DEVELOPMENT ISSUES LOBBYIST

All trends indicate that positions as lobbyists in the new century will become plentiful for energetic, political, and humanistic people.

California-Based Advocacy Group

Founded in 1971, the California Children's Lobby, a subscriber-supported public interest organization, is an example of an organization dedicated to providing a non-partisan voice for children. Sherry Skelly is one of the organization's lobbyists. According to Sherry, three key words—Children, Education, and Politics—motivated her to enter this new field.

Sherry worked in the child care field as an extended day teacher while she was an undergraduate. When she decided to go back to school, she majored in political science, after which she did an internship with a consumer group, developing processes for contacting and dealing with legislators.

While attending the California university system schools, Sherry became aware of the lack of child care centers at the university campuses. In 1987 she approached the governor's office and began lobbying for this important project. Today, many of the university system schools now boast child care centers.

Now employed by the California Children's Lobby, Sherry works as a children's lobbyist. The Children's Lobby has acted as a catalyst for the enactment of new laws for children—laws on child abuse, child health, child development, foster care, adoption, and more. Each of these laws has made a difference for thousands of children in California.

For further information on this advocacy group, contact:

CALIFORNIA CHILDREN'S LOBBY
926 J St.
Sacramento, CA 95814
(916) 443-1096

Nationwide Advocacy Group

Nationally, the Children's Defense Fund is one of the largest organizations speaking out for children's causes. This group is particularly interested in giving attention to the needs of poor, minority, and disabled children. The group pursues a legislative agenda in the United States Congress and litigates selected cases of major importance.

Those in the child care field are grateful to this organization for the passage of the ABC Bill, now known as the Child Care Block Grant Bill. Monies from this bill are now being disbursed to the states.

For more information, contact:

CHILDREN'S DEFENSE FUND
122 C St. NW
Washington, DC 20001
(202) 628-8787

Other Organizations Dedicated to Social Reform and Children

Several organizations across the nation are dedicated to changing and improving our society. Many of these organizations offer a variety of job opportunities, especially for young people or students who are interested in working as interns.

Again, check with your local Child Care Resource and Referral Agency for organizations in your area. Following are four of these organizations:

FOR LOVE OF CHILDREN (FLOC)
1711 14th St. NW
Washington, DC 20009
(202) 462-8686

(Dedicated to helping abused and neglected children by advocating changes in government policy, helping and finding families for the children, and assisting with education and other needs for shelters.)

FRANKLIN COMMUNITY ACTION CORPORATION
39 Federal St.
Greenfield, MA 01301
(413) 774-2318

(Assists children from low-income families in the area with after-school care, day care, and youth centers.)

UNITED COMMUNITIES AGAINST POVERTY
1400 Doewood Lane
Capitol Heights, MD 20743
(301) 322-5700

(Dedicated to improving health, education, training, and housing for low-income families in the area; has an emphasis on early childhood development.)

PLANNED PARENTHOOD FEDERATION OF AMERICA, INC.
810 7th Ave.
New York, NY 10019
(212) 541-7800

(National organization providing medical, educational, and counseling services to meet family planning needs; acts in social and legislative advocacy capacity to ensure reproductive freedom.)

11. Role of the Child Care Advocate

Advocacy in the child care field means speaking out or taking action on behalf of our children as well as our child care workers. When you enter this field, you will be taking part in decisions that affect government and community directions in child care. Since children cannot represent themselves, you will be protecting their interests.

"WORTHY WORK... WORTHLESS WAGES"

The time has come for overworked child care personnel to work in educating the public about child care work values and the skills necessary to perform quality child care. The Child Care Employee Project coined this noteworthy phrase: "Worthy Work—Worthless Wages."

The National Child Care Staffing Study, conducted by the Child Care Employee Project, documented the nationwide staffing crisis by studying 227 child care centers in Boston, Atlanta, Detroit, Phoenix, and Seattle. The centers selected for study represented the diversity of center-based care throughout the country. Here are some of the major findings as taken from the Executive Summary:

- The education of child care teaching staff and the arrangement of their work environment are essential determinants of the quality of services children receive.
- The teaching staff provides more sensitive and appropriate caregiving if they have completed several years of formal education, received college level early childhood training, earned higher wages and better benefits, and worked in centers devoting a higher percentage of the operating budget to teaching personnel.
- The most important predictor of the quality of care children receive is staff wages.
- The quality of service provided by most of the centers was barely adequate. Higher quality centers have higher wages, better work environment, lower staff turnover, lower child/staff ratio, and better educated and trained staff.
- The better quality centers were more likely to be operated on a non-profit basis, were accredited by the NAEYC, were located

118 ■ CAREERS IN CHILD CARE

in states with higher quality standards, and were meeting child/staff ratios, group size, and staff training provisions contained in the 1980 Federal Interagency Day Care (FIDC) requirements.
- Despite having higher levels of formal education than the average American worker, child care teaching staff earn lower wages. ... The predominantly female work force earns an average hourly wage of $5.35. ... In the last decade, child care staff wages, when adjusted for inflation, have decreased more than 20 percent. ... Child care teaching staff earn less than half as much as comparably educated women and less than one-third as much as comparably educated men in the civilian work force.
- Staff turnover has nearly tripled in the last decade, jumping from 15 percent in 1977 to 41 percent in 1988. ... The most important determinant of staff turnover was staff wages. ... Teaching staff earning the lowest wages are twice as likely to leave their jobs as those earning the highest wages. ... Children attending lower-quality centers and centers with high staff turnover were less competent in language and social development.
- Children from low and high income families were more likely to attend centers providing higher quality care than were children from middle income families.
- Compared with a decade ago, child care centers in the United States receive fewer governmental funds, care for a larger number of infants, and are more likely to be operated on a for-profit basis.

Recommendations

- Raise child care teaching staff salaries as a means of recruiting and retaining qualified child care workers.
- Promote formal education and training opportunities for child care teaching staff to improve their ability to interact effectively with children and to create developmentally appropriate environments.
- Adopt state and federal standards for child/staff ratios, staff education, training, and compensation in order to raise the floor of quality in America's child care centers.
- Develop industry standards to minimize the disparities in quality among types of child care programs.
- Promote public education about the importance of adequately trained and compensated teaching staff in child care programs in order to secure support for the full cost of care.

In their policy statement, the National Association for the Education of Young Children (NAEYC) acknowledges that the quality of care that children receive is directly affected by the working conditions of the child caregivers. The battle cry for child care workers in the '90s is to raise public awareness about the plight of our child care workers. Thus, we can rest assured that children, who are our nation's greatest resources, will be protected and cared for in a safe and an affordable manner.

Along with the downside of child care also comes optimism and opportunity. Although many challenges are facing the child care field, there are wonderful rewards in personal fulfillment and close relationships with youngsters and their families. In a sense, you will be playing a major role in the growth and development of children while creating a bond with other staff and professionals in the field.

TEN STEPS FOR BECOMING AN ON-THE-JOB CHILD CARE WORKER'S ADVOCATE

1. Read and review the National Child Care Staffing Study. Disseminate this information to legislators, parent groups, policy makers, and the general public.
2. Promote the changing of unclear job descriptions, which lead to resentment over pay and titles.
3. Attend board meetings and encourage staff representation on the board.
4. Ask to review policies and programs. Learn about the center's corporate structure.
5. Clarify the decision-making power. For example, does the staff have input on what toys need purchasing?
6. Verbalize and acknowledge such issues as how low pay and lack of benefits create low morale or how stress affects the job.
7. Advocacy helps child care staff help themselves.
8. Help parents understand how low wages affect the care of their children.
9. Inform legislators that the low wages and high staff turnover found in most child care centers will affect the quality of care.
10. Consider unionizing. Forming a union gives workers the right to bargain with their employers on the conditions of their employment. In addition to wages, a union contract covers such issues as job security, adequate time breaks, classroom preparation time, and manageable child/staff ratios.

For more information on raising teacher's salaries and unionizing, contact:

CHILD CARE EMPLOYEE PROJECT
6536 Telegraph Ave., Suite A-201
Oakland, CA 94609
(415) 653-9889

"Never doubt that a small group of thoughtful, committed citizens can change the world. Indeed, it's the only thing that ever has." — Margaret Mead

CHILD CARE AND DEVELOPMENT BLOCK GRANT

In the fall of 1990, Congress adopted a monumental piece of child care legislation titled, "Child Care and Development Block Grant." Child care advocates are to be congratulated on this truly historic victory. The enactment of federal child care legislation is not only a critical step forward for children and their families, it also sets the stage for training programs and improving salaries for child care staff who provide child care services under this act. Here's what the 1990 Act provides: (1) $2.5 billion of new federal child care block grants over the next three years; (2) provisions to protect children receiving care; (3) $1.5 billion over five years to help low-income families who are at risk of becoming dependent on welfare-purchased child care; and (4) $18.2 billion in tax relief for low-income working families.

A public thank-you is in order for Marian Wright Edelman, Executive Director, Children's Defense Fund, a twenty-year veteran in child care advocacy who worked long and hard for the passage of this bill.

Advocacy also involves watching the implementation of the 1990 Act. The block grant federal monies have been allocated to address the issues of child care affordability, accessibility, and quality. Watch for the answers to these questions: How will the funds be allocated? Will they be funded to the State Department of Education in each state? Or will the funds go directly to the local governments and agencies?

The Act says that states must offer eligible parents certificates to help them pay for the child care of their choice. In turn, the states must also give child care providers grants or contracts to offer subsidized care.

Watch what activities are used to improve quality and accessibility. With 20 percent of the reserved funds allocated for quality improvement activities, will this improvement mean a raise in salaries for child care workers?

SECTION II
WORKING WITH CHILDREN AND FAMILIES

Section II is dedicated to the new teacher who has made the career decision to work directly with children. Since this is a career exploration book, this section is included to make your transition into child care somewhat easier.

Written as a practical guide, you'll find a multitude of curriculum ideas and fun activities. Use these ideas as starting points, then use your own creativity to adapt the activities to your own child care environment.

Knowing what interests young children and what their limitations are will help you plan activities that will enhance each child's development. Begin forming partnerships with your children and soon you'll learn what approach is right for you.

The curriculum for preschoolers has been emphasized in Chapter 12 mostly because the majority of caregivers will fall into this group. Many of the activities listed in this section can be adapted to other age levels.

Note to parents: This section also serves as an aid to parents. After reading the section on child care curriculum, you will have a better understanding about your child's day care activities and what to look for in selecting a quality program that meets your child's needs.

12. Curriculum Guide for Caregivers

THE KEY TO EFFECTIVE CHILD CARE

All caregivers, whether they are working in a home or center, have a common bond—they want to provide a learning and nurturing environment for children. Written especially for new teachers and caregivers, this chapter will help you survive the trials and tribulations of working with groups of children.

Curriculum planning holds the key for incorporating your philosophies and objectives. Curriculum activities offer meaningful experiences for children. They learn from these planned experiences by doing and exploring for themselves. Sometimes adults have a difficult time understanding that children learn through play. For children, play is "work." By observing youngsters at play, teachers learn more about children and their joys, fears, and interests.

In essence, caregivers form lasting relationships with children and their families. These relationships encourage a certain amount of uniqueness and give you a method of measuring your success.

The curriculum suggestions in this chapter will help you in your work with children of all ages. Whatever the age, always remember that building confidence and self-esteem are more important for preschool children than making them learn the alphabet or their numbers. Children not only learn from play and activities, they learn by interacting with other children.

WORKING WITH INFANTS AND TODDLERS

Newborn to 12 Months

Those who choose to care for infants are embarking on an exciting experience. Infant care takes a special, loving type of person. A helpless human being at birth, an infant relies on you to fulfill all his basic needs. An infant experiences a variety of emotions—anger, fear, contentment, distress. By six months your infant charge begins exploring his environment, and amazingly by 12-15 months he has his hands on everything. He begins using muscle power to discover his universe.

Toddler (Ages 12-24 months)

From ages 12 to 24 months, children learn very quickly about themselves and their world. Toddlers are curious, demanding, egocentric, lovable, and moody. This age group spends a good deal of their time developing motor skills. They are crawling, walking, pushing, looking, feeling, and tasting. Give them plenty of room to explore their environment safely. Introduce toddlers to their world by allowing them to use their five senses.

Teachers of toddlers need patience, energy, and creativity. These youngsters have short attention spans, so keep their activities and toys as simple as possible. Most of all, toddlers need love, hugs, and praise from their caregivers.

Encouraging Physical, Emotional, Social, and Intellectual Development

As an infant/toddler caregiver you'll want to encourage development. Here are several suggestions for meeting an infant or toddler's physical, emotional, social, and intellectual development: For social and emotional development, cuddle, hold and play with infants. Babies develop rapidly when they're actively involved in social activities with adults. Talk or sing to baby while feeding and diapering. This fosters intellectual development. Make his world interesting and responsive by changing toys and activities. Baby-proof the baby's environment to keep him or her safe and to make your supervision easier. Since the danger of injuries is high at this stage, always remember to protect the infant from harm. Play simple games with the baby. The three big B's are favorites—balls, books, and blocks. The smaller the child, the bigger the ball. A variety of good books is available for babies. Simple blocks can be made from a variety of materials such as foam covered with soft fabric.

Show excitement and joy when the baby learns a new skill. Talk to the baby about what she is doing. Babies are sensitive to the tone of your voice and will soon respond to single words such as "hot" or "bye-bye." Provide comfort when baby is fussy or not feeling well. Rocking or playing music sometimes offers comfort. Allow the baby freedom to explore and discover the world on his own. Little ones enjoy emptying and refilling the same container; this activity teaches them how things work.

Games for Infants/Toddlers

Newborn to 3 Months: Hang mobiles, balloons, or ribbons over the bassinet or crib. Introduce new sounds to the baby—music, bells, wind chimes, a ticking clock. Hold a rattle or noise maker above the baby's head. Shake the rattle, and when the baby sees it, move it slowly around in a circle. Change the direction of the circle.

3 to 6 Months: Provide baby with a variety of safe crib toys—rattles, cuddly animals, teething toys, baby mirrors. Make sure the toys are lightweight and in different shapes. Babies like to feel different textures. Make your own "feely" blanket with patches of different fabrics—velvet, fur, lace, plastic vinyl, dotted swiss, or rubber. Find safe household objects of different sizes, shapes, and textures for baby. Keep these objects handy; when she becomes bored with one, give her another.

6 to 12 Months: Fasten small toys to the baby's crib or high chair, and let him enjoy swinging or flinging the objects. Children at this age love all types of household containers — cardboard boxes, oatmeal boxes, empty cans with safe edges, hard plastic containers or lightweight plastic bowls. Make a tunnel for baby to crawl through, either by knocking out the ends of a large cardboard box or by piling cushions on the floor.

12 to 24 Months: Go for a walk through the neighborhood and have the toddlers gather small items to put in a box. Back in the classroom, have the children glue their items (feathers, Popsicle sticks, rocks, etc.) to heavy paper. Have them talk about how each item feels. Toddlers particularly enjoy water, so put together a plastic dishpan, sponges, pot scrubbers, and small plastic dishes. Put the items in the water and let the toddlers explain how they feel. Collect small containers such as 35mm film containers and fill them with a variety of items (dried rice, dried beans, small bells, etc.). Show the toddler how to shake them and listen for the different sounds.

PRESCHOOLER'S GROWTH AND DEVELOPMENT

Emotional/Social Development

Young children are in continuous growing patterns. By providing a nurturing, consistent, secure environment, children develop a sense of trust and understanding. Preschoolers experience pleasure, particularly when they master a new skill. They also learn about anger, such as when another child knocks down his block tower. As a teacher, you will need to allow each child to express his or her feelings, both negative and positive. Children gain self-esteem and learn best when someone talks *with* them, not *at* them.

Children need opportunities to develop relationships with other children. From these relationships, they learn to respect the feelings of their peers.

Physical/Motor Development

Since preschoolers run and climb with ease, keep their physical/motor skills in mind. Children learn through body action. They thrive in an environment that provides water play, sand box play, and wheel toys on a solid surface. By developing an understanding of themselves in space, children learn about the limits of their bodies. They need a play/learning classroom that allows them to move freely yet controls out-of-bounds behavior. As a teacher, you will need to keep your classroom safe, clean, and comfortable, thereby helping foster each child's growth.

Intellectual/Cognitive Development

Because each child is a unique individual, create opportunities for each of your preschoolers to explore the classroom environment at his or her own pace. When setting your classroom goals, allow children to think and solve problems, enjoy and feel successful at learning, and use music and language for expressing their creativity. Fill their days with exciting play experiences.

PRESCHOOL CURRICULUM PLANNING

As our society changes, effective teachers learn to adapt their curriculum in such a manner that preschoolers can discover and use it in their present world. Children should learn to manipulate things and to develop feelings, so that they can affect and control their environment.

The suggestions outlined in this chapter are designed to help the child organize the reality around him in a meaningful way. As a teacher you can help the child connect what he learns to what is important and what matters to him.

Strive to be creative with your ideas, and vary the programs in a manner that excites you. No one wants to experience the boredom that comes about by following the same old routine. Children sense your enthusiasm for a new experience.

Themes may be helpful in organizing your curriculum. When planning around themes, take into consideration the children's physical, social, and intellectual needs. The following themes are divided into topics for the school year (September to June).

September	Self-awareness; who am I? All about me (books) Sorting and classifying objects
October	Seasons; changes in weather Colors: black and orange Halloween holiday
November	Winter preparations Harvest/Thanksgiving Pilgrims and Indians Colors: Yellow, green and blue

December	Around the world holidays Shapes: rectangle, square, and circle Transportation: trains, cars, airplanes
January	Community helpers: police officers, fire fighters Martin Luther King, Jr.'s birthday
February	President's birthdays Valentine's Day Post Office Black history month
March	Weather: rain, snow, wind, clouds St. Patrick's Day Color: green
April	Growing: seeds, plantings Farm animals
May	Circus Flowers and insects Mother's Day
June	Vacations Seashore animals and fish Father's Day

HOW PRESCHOOLERS LEARN BY USING THE FIVE SENSES

Preschoolers are beginning to use their five senses—tasting, seeing, smelling, hearing, and touching. As a child uses his senses, he learns about the world on his own. For example, a preschooler learns about grass by feeling the grass, by crawling through the grass, and by smelling and tasting it. The young child doesn't know the meaning behind "the grass is green" or "the grass is rough."

To help children understand their senses, display pictures of children using their five senses in everyday experiences. For example, use five separate papers with large drawings, each acting as a symbol for this poem:

> Two eyes to see
> Two ears to hear
> One tongue to taste
> Two hands to feel
> One nose to smell.

Cooking is a good way for children to use all five senses. It's also useful for learning mathematical concepts and for increasing their vocabulary.

Smell

The four primary smells are fragrant, acid, rancid, and burnt. Much of what we taste is really what we smell. Talk about the smell of classroom items such as clay or paint. Use a fragrant room deodorizer and guess what it smells like. Put peppermint or oil of cloves in playdough.

Blindfold Game: Display different types of items such as perfumes, onions, mint leaves, garlic, pipe tobacco, and coffee. Have the children see and taste some of the items (not the tobacco, of course), then blindfold them to see if they can guess which smell goes with which item.

Craft: Use fruits and vegetables that smell (lemons, apples, potatoes, carrots) for block printing. Have the child dip these items in paint, then transfer them to paper.

Taste

Children can learn about the four types of primary tastes. The front of the tongue senses salt and sweet; the sides of the tongue detect sour; and the back of the tongue tastes bitterness. Most foods are a combination of all four. Most food flavors, however, are recognized through the sense of smell. During juice time, place a pinch of salt and a pinch of sugar on each child's napkin. Salt and sugar look alike and have no smell, so they have to be tasted to tell them apart. Children also enjoy using hand juicers to make their own juice.

Blindfold Game: Select a variety of cut-up foods such as bananas, apples, pineapple, and popcorn. Have each child guess what he is tasting.

Field Trip: Visit a local bakery. Children can use their five senses—seeing, smelling, tasting, touching the cookies, and hearing. (The bread slicer makes an interesting sound.)

Hearing

Hearing is one of our most important senses. It gives us pleasure, and it warns us of danger. Also, hearing is vital to communication, socialization, and intellectual and emotional development. Through the sense of hearing you can help children discover new sounds, understand the sounds they know, and discriminate between sounds such as city noises, nature sounds, and manmade sounds.

Tape Recorder: Use a tape recorder in class. Children love to hear their own voices. Tape their playtime for fun, too.

Stories: Read stories about sound (*The Indoor Noisy Book, Loudest*

Noise in the World or *Roar and More*.) Some of these sounds help eliminate a child's fears.

Crafts: Make a walkie-talkie out of two juice cans with holes in the bottom and about five feet of wire or nylon string held taut. Have one child talk and another one listen. Make noisemakers by putting beans inside two paper plates and stapling them together. Children enjoy painting or decorating these tambourines. Tie small bells to yarn for another type of noisemaker.

Listening Walk: First read *Listening Walk* by P. Showers, then go on a noise hunt outside. Have each child tell you something he hears: cars honking, sounds of cars, garbage can lids, airplanes, dogs barking, people's voices. After they return to the classroom, have them make familiar sounds such as the telephone ringing, a clock ticking, or water running.

Mystery Sounds Game: This game helps children listen and recognize sounds. While the others watch, blindfold one child and make a noise: hold a clock by his ear, move a chair, pour water, tear paper, drop a pencil, bounce a ball, or shut the door.

Sight

Children take a giant learning step when they begin looking closely at the world around them. This is an important way to learn. Children can learn to develop their visual sense through everyday experiences. During a walk, ask, "Who sees the blue car?" or "I see a truck. Who can find another truck?" In the grocery store with a small group of three or four children, you might say, "I see something we use to make sandwiches. It is wrapped in blue and white paper. Can you find it?" or "Can you find what we drink at lunch that's wrapped in a white carton?"

Cooking: Cooking experiences help the senses of seeing and tasting. Crack an egg, show the children the shell and how it fits together. Show them the egg white and the yolk in a bowl. Talk about what parts of foods they eat (egg white and yolk, orange and grapefruit sections) and what parts they don't eat (eggshells, orange peels, carrot tops).

Changing Sight: Demonstrate the use of binoculars, kaleidoscopes, magnifying glasses, and small telescopes. Discuss the differences. Have the children make and decorate a telescope out of toilet tissue rolls. Have the children look into a mirror, then close their eyes and look again. Talk about the changes in the size of the pupil and eye colors. Children like to compare likes and differences. ("Scott has blue eyes, Rachel's eyes are brown.")

Light Game: Have a child hold a flashlight on the palm of his or her hand and look at the bones.

Game: Prepare a tray of small objects: pen, pencil, eraser, chalk, button, penny, crayon, etc., and cover them with a cloth or paper. Remove the cover for a few seconds while the children look at the objects. Replace the cover and ask the children to tell you what they saw.

Touch

Through touch, children learn many things they couldn't learn any other way. As mentioned earlier, a preschooler learns about grass by feeling the grass, not by being told about it. Display a variety of contrasting textures, such as raw rice, clay, play dough, sand, cornmeal, water, and liquid starch, and have the children feel the differences.

Feel the Object Game: Children particularly enjoy this game. Show all the children the objects that are going into a box or drawstring bag (wooden block, piece of soft fur, cotton, rubber ball, piece of plastic, etc.). Call each child individually to pick something out of the bag with his eyes closed and try to identify it.

Feel Book: Make a feel book with cardboard. Children like about four or five pages tied together with some colorful string. Some of the objects for a feel book may include: furs, feathers, Styrofoam or plastic pieces, different sizes and textures of buttons, rubber bands, foil, cotton, and sandpaper.

FIVE AREAS OF CLASSROOM FOCUS

Preschool children need activities that stimulate their interest yet prepare them for school. Essentially, there are five areas of curriculum development—art, music, science, math, and language arts.

Art

The process of art is really more important than the product itself. Many art activities have the potential of developing thinking skills. Paper is a good example. As children work with paper, they learn its properties by coloring it, painting it, cutting it, and tearing it.

Painting teaches about different forms. A child's cognition is fostered by offering several methods of painting — brushes, sponges, string, cotton swabs and, best of all, the child's fingers.

Clay is a good medium for the development of perceptual motor skills. The child's tactile awareness of clay stimulates awareness as he or she smooths it, rolls it around, or squeezes it through the fingers. Clay is perceived as something that responds to commands. From these experiences a child learns to shape an idea. For example, in one classroom a four year old molded three objects into squares. As the class began to interact, he said, "These are gravestones." What a marvelous idea he shared by recalling an experience of visiting a cemetery with his parents. People, places, and things come to the forefront of a child's thinking process as he or she replicates images in a three-dimensional medium.

Play Dough Recipe (uncooked):
4 cups flour
2 cups salt
1 cup warm water with few drops food coloring added

Mix the flour and salt. Slowly stir in the water to a kneading consistency. Add two drops vegetable oil and stir.

Store in a plastic bag in the refrigerator. To reuse, roll the dough in a small amount of flour.

Music

Music is multi-faceted. It is motion, sound, rhythm, singing, and playing instruments. Music is the teacher's golden opportunity to assist children in their creative development.

Singing should be enjoyed without making it competitive. The goal is to have fun and receive satisfaction.

In planning creative rhythmic movement, teachers need not be musicians. By using a rhythmic beat, simple rhymes, and a creative atmosphere, children can be led into musical activities that will help them become well-integrated beings.

The concepts of space, distance, and size are learned by sensory stimulation—stimulation through movement and muscle use. Through movement, children learn about postural adjustment directions and eye-hand coordination, and that they have two hands and two feet. Movement includes dancing. In order for a child to dance, he or she needs to explore space, dynamics, and sound.

Appropriate Songs for Preschool Children:
"Where is _____ (child's name)?"
(To the tune of "Frere Jacques")
    Where is Tracy (or child's name)?
    Where is Tracy? Teacher points to child.
    Here I am. Child gets up from seat.
    Here I am. There she is. Teacher and other children sing.
    There she is.
    How are you today? Teacher sings.
    How are you today?
    Very well thank you.
    Very well thank you.
    Teacher begins with another student.

"Twinkle, Twinkle Little Star"
    Twinkle, twinkle little star
    How I wonder what you are
    Up above the world so high
    Like a diamond in the sky
    Twinkle, twinkle little star
    How I wonder what you are.

"Ring Around the Roses"
   (Teacher and students form a circle, holding hands.)
   Ring around the roses,
   Pockets full of posies,
   Ashes, ashes
   We all fall down!
   (Teacher and students fall to the ground.)

Science

As young children watch, wonder, study, and question, they are integrating science into their everyday living. Teachers can help children develop concepts that will keep them safe from the hazards within their environment. Children should be taught that they need air to breathe. Spiders help our gardens, but some spiders can hurt us. Ice on the pond may not support our weight, and we must keep away from moving cars and trucks.

Curriculum for science includes many aspects of our environment —plants, animals, rocks, tools, machinery, and the atmosphere.

Sample Lesson Plan: What is air?

Hold up your hands to make a picture frame. Show the children that air is invisible. Explain in simple terms that air is part of the earth, not a separate entity. Air is inside a balloon. When air blows, it's called "wind." Have a child blow through a straw and feel the air on his/her hands.

Air is real. Put a handkerchief or tissue into a glass. Insert the glass straight down into a bowl of water; withdraw it quickly, straight up. Air keeps the handkerchief or tissue dry. Then put the glass straight down and tilt it to one side. The bubbles of air will escape and water will enter the glass.

Air can be poured. Lower one glass into a tank of water and let it fill with water; lower another glass mouth down, so the air cannot escape until it is under the first glass. Tilt the second glass slightly. The air escapes from the second glass and replaces the water out of the first glass. Air can be "poured."

Air has weight. Take a clean straw, hold a finger over the top, and place the straw in a glass of water. No water will enter. The finger keeps air in the straw and prevents water from entering. Remove the finger and watch water enter the straw. Replace the finger on top of the straw and lift it up. Water will stay in the straw because air is pressing on the lower end.

Air lifts. Have a child inhale from a straw while another child holds a piece of tissue paper. The child will be able to lift paper with a straw. Place a paper sack under a book and blow air into the sack so it lifts the book.

Air presses. During snack time puncture one hole only in a juice can. Show the children how the juice comes out slowly. Next, puncture a second hole and observe how the air goes into the upper hole and forces the juice out at a faster rate.

Water goes into air. Wet a blackboard or the sidewalk outside and watch it dry. Put water into different sized jars and watch the different evaporation rates.

Air is strong. Have a child run a few steps with a piece of cardboard in front of his face. He will feel the cardboard pushing against something. This is air. Have a child run with a paper sack open. The sack will fill with air. Close it like a balloon and make it go "pop."

Math

The preschool environment is rich in geometric experiences. You can begin helping children learn mathematical reasoning by talking with the children and allowing them "hands-on" experience with the following shapes: Sphere—balls, marbles, bubbles, beads; Cylinder—oatmeal boxes, cans, pipes, straws; Circle—dishes, rings, wheels; Arc—when you swing, when you open a door, when you kick; Angle—corners, knees, elbows, noses, heels, hands on a clock; Cube—blocks, ice cubes, sugar cubes, some boxes; Rectangle — doors, walls, ceilings, floors, windows, books; Cone—ice cream cones, funnels, megaphones, pine cones, tops; Square—floor tiles, checkerboards, sidewalk squares; Torus—doughnut, tire, Cheerio, pool toys.

Other Math Concepts: Sets—a bunch of grapes, a pocket full of pebbles, a table full of dishes. One-to-One Matching—choosing a partner, passing out cookies, sitting in chairs, putting a brush in a paint jar. Counting—match a set of numbers to a set of things: 1 and 2 to Latisha (1) and Brittany (2); you have two (2) friends. Greater than—one set of crayons has more crayons than another set; when I am 4 and you are 3. Less than—when there are fewer girls than boys; when I have fewer toys than you have. Names of numbers—the way we tell how many: English—one, two, three; Spanish—uno, dos, tres.

Language Arts

Language arts, a part of daily living, is functional in every activity and experience. Speaking, listening, reading and writing are interrelated, and corresponding skills are developed as the child participates in varied activities throughout the day.

Creative dramatics should be stressed in the preschool environment. Creative dramatics center around episodes and relationships that are significant to the children. Through this type of play, they reveal themselves and their concepts of the world.

Family dramas are the ones most frequently reenacted. Children want to understand what it is like to be grownup and to do grownup things. In their play they prepare themselves for these roles.

The values of dramatic play are significant. Dramatic play gives children a sense of control in various situations. They can play-act experiences that are disturbing or frightening. They have an opportunity to draw off negative feelings.

Experiences with books and storytelling should be part of the daily program for preschool children. Desirable books will include familiar, everyday subjects. They should be short and written in simple, correct English with clear, colorful illustrations. *Are You My Mother?* by P.D. Eastman is a good example of a book popular with four year olds. In the book a baby bird searches for his mother. During the search, he encounters many familiar things—cat, hen, dog, cow, boat, and steam shovel.

You might want to post the following anonymous poem:

"You may have tangible wealth untold
Caskets of jewels, coppers of gold,
But richer than I you will never be
For I had someone who told stories to me."

All-Time Favorite Stories:

Love You Forever by Robert Munsch (A little boy grows up in a loving family to become a father himself)

Madeline by Ludwig Bemelmans (12 little girls and their adventures in Paris)

The Story of Babar by Jean De Brunhoff (The adventures of a little elephant coming from the jungle to the big city, including a wedding celebration)

Curious George by H.A. Rey (An adventure story about a monkey and his friend, a man with a yellow hat)

The Cat in the Hat by Dr. Seuss (An amusing story about the tricks of a cat)

Millions of Cats by Wanda Gag (An old man sets out to find his wife and brings home all the cats he finds)

The Carrot Seed by Crockett Johnston (A boy plants a seed and waits for it to come up)

The Noisy Book by Margaret Wise Brown (A book about sounds)

Where the Wild Things Are by Maurice Sendak (A boy's dreams of animals and how he tames them)

Are You My Mother? by P.D. Eastman (A baby bird searches for his mother)

The Snowy Day by Ezra Jack Keats (The story of a small boy in the snow)

Where's Waldo? by Martin Handford (Search and find illustrations and story about Waldo)

Caps for Sale by Esthyl Slobodkina (A tale about a peddler, some monkeys, and their "monkey business")

Swimmy by Leo Lionni (A fish organizes a school of fish so they can outwit a bully fish)

The Little Engine That Could retold by Watty Piper (A story about the patience and persistence of a little engine getting up a hill)

Favorite Classics:
Three Billy Goat's Gruff
The Three Bears
The Little Red Hen
The Gingerbread Man
Chicken Little
That's What Friends are For by Frances Heide and Sylvia Van Clief (An elephant gets hurt in the forest and needs to meet his cousin. The forest friends give advice.)

CURRICULUM FOR SCHOOL-AGE CHILDREN

Once you understand the needs of school-age children, you can plan programs that support growth and learning. School-age children like to compete with each other, against themselves, and act out real life situations.

School-age children let adults know in a variety of ways that they like to be in control; they question authority. Therefore, as a school-age teacher, you will need to be flexible, a good listener, and work to develop a friendship with the child.

A well-balanced program for this age level will include arts, crafts, sports, and outdoor activities. Also, include the children in your planning. Find out what they like to do and respect their decisions.

If you are working with five-year-old children who are making the big transition into "real" school, you will find that their needs are different from the older school-age child. Three important characteristics of the five year old are: they want individual time with their caregivers; they are active in their small and large muscle play; and they glamorize the outside world and spend time fantasizing their role.

Caregivers need to remember that at this age children have already spent three or more hours in another program, so they'll need new activities and interests to keep them from getting bored. Sometimes they're tired when they arrive at your program. They may need a nap, especially after morning kindergarten.

Because five year olds are in a constant state of flux, their entire day should not be scheduled. Instead, these children need to make decisions and choices to become their own people.

Five year olds need materials related to their imaginative role playing—building blocks; dress-up clothes; super hero toys; and props for acting out TV plots.

Activities

Following are some of the activities that interest school-age children:

- Adopt a classroom pet, grandparent, tree, etc.
- Undertake an insect project such as raising butterflies or moths.
- Set up a woodworking project. Children derive great pleasure from pounding nails into wood. Make a boat, an airplane, or a bird house, for example.
- Start a collection — postcards, rocks, seashells, dolls, or buttons, for example.
- Plan for a time of bird watching. Find out about the different types of birds. What's the biggest, the smallest?
- Learn and teach the children magic tricks.
- Plan a variety of arts and crafts programs — clay modeling, photo montage, string art, or tie-dyeing, for example.
- Provide a variety of games: 20 questions; I Spy; board games (checkers, chess, Monopoly); card games; outdoor games (hide and seek, tag, jumprope); paper/pencil games (tic-tac toe, crosswords); and ball games such as baseball.

CLASSROOM ENVIRONMENTS

Day care programs vary widely in terms of classroom structures. However, quality programs provide children with many choices in materials. Time and space have been clearly developed in constructive ways. As teacher, you are available for support and requests from children for materials and activities.

The day care environment almost resembles a three-ring circus — one small group of children may be playing in the block corner, another group listening to stories, and another creating works of art at the play dough table. They move from one area and project to another independently. At some time during the day, you will draw the children into a large group for sharing and singing.

In order to create a quality environment within the classroom, you will need to have most of the following materials and supplies:

Animals	Crayons
Balls	Dolls and accessories
Blocks	Easels
Books	Filmstrips
Climbing apparatus (jungle gym)	Fingerpaints
	Housekeeping toys
Collage materials	Jumpropes
Cooking materials	Lockers or cubbies

Math materials (abacus, number games)
Manipulative toys (take aparts, Legos®, geo-boards)
Musical instruments
Phonograph
Piano
Program materials
Puppets
Puzzles
Riding equipment (tricycles, wagons, cars)
Running water
Sand and appropriate toys
Science materials
Slides
Store equipment
Stuffed animals
Swings
Table games
Water play area
Woodworking materials

13. Multicultural, Anti-bias Curriculum

Single parent children, poor children, handicapped children, and children whose parents are lesbian or gay . . . This diversity is the characteristic of the changing family of today. We will likely see even more family transformations during the next decade.

Fewer than 10 percent of today's families conform to the "Ozzie and Harriet" image of a full-time, stay-at-home mother and a full-time breadwinning father raising two or more children. The number of single-parent families has doubled in the last twenty years, and nearly half of the children born today will live in a single-parent home for some portion of their lives.

Because of the diversity of families now and in the future, it's important for caregivers to understand multi-cultural values and understand anti-bias principles. In her book, *Home Centered Care: Designing a Family Day Care Program*, author Rhonda Garcia explains the purpose of providing multi-cultural experiences for young children. "The feeling of pride in one's own lifestyle and one's own way of thinking is a powerful influence in helping children view themselves as worthwhile and valued human beings. Caregivers have a responsibility to model positive attitudes toward all children. A child's first idea of herself or himself as a person depends upon the responses of others. As caregivers you are in a position to provide support to parent(s) while they are educating their young children about who they are and how they relate to their community, city, and country.

There are significant reasons why providing multi-cultural experiences for young children is important:
1. To make children feel good about who they are irrespective of their nationality or race.
2. To share cultural diversity with other children so that they may respect and appreciate cultures different from their own."

When planning activities for young children, remember that multi-cultural curriculum differs from anti-bias curriculum in its approach. Multi-cultural curriculum is intended to teach children about each other's cultures, while anti-bias curriculum teaches an understanding and tolerance of other family styles and cultures.

Unfortunately, many teachers emphasize "tourism curriculum."

That is, they teach about another culture only through celebrations and through food, clothing, and housing. For example, Mexican-American life is usually celebrated one day a year on Cinco de Mayo, Jewish life on Chanukah, and black culture on Martin Luther King's birthday. Although these are important events and one method for introducing new ideas, they are sometimes patronizing and trivial. They don't necessarily deal with the real life picture (problems and experiences) of different people and their cultures.

CLASSROOM ACTIVITIES

To make your program culturally diverse and to reduce prejudice, begin discussing diversities in a natural way. For example, when discussing different races, talk with the children about their skin, hair, and eye colors. Have the children look at themselves and others in a large mirror. Make a special book for each child, showing pictures of him or her at a favorite activity. You may want the parents to contribute other pictures of their families — grandparents, aunts, uncles, and cousins. From these books, you can begin a discussion of how people come in all different colors, shapes, and sizes.

For example, when talking with a young black child, notice that his or her skin is dark brown. You can say, "Dark brown and black are beautiful colors." Tell the child to be proud of him/herself. There is a book titled *Black is Beautiful*. Read this book to the children. *Whistle for Willie* is the title of another children's book that deals with self-esteem.

Have the Hispanic child introduce a Spanish song and help the other children learn to count to ten in Spanish.

Play culturally diverse music to the children.

Display pictures on the classroom walls that include people of different cultures. If possible, take a field trip to an area rich in cultural diversity such as Chinatown or Koreatown.

Suggested Books

Following is a list of several good books that address the diversity of families and deal with disabilities:

Interracial Families:
Black is Brown is Tan by A. Adoff
Living in Two Worlds by M. Rosenberg

Black Families:
Ten, Nine, Eight by M. Bang
Don't You Remember? by L. Clifton
Black is Beautiful by A. McGovern
Honey, I Love You by E. Greenfield
Yaga Days by C. Martel

Hispanic Families:
What Do I Do? Que Hago by N. Simon
Friday Night is Paps Night by R. Sonneborn
The Goat in the Rug by C. Bood and M. Link
I Am Here/Yo Estoy Aqui by R. Blue

Asian Families:
Umbrella by T. Yashima
Straight Hair, Curly Hair by A. Goldin
The Iron Moonhunter by K. Chang
First Snow by H. Constant

Native-American Families:
The Paper Crane by M. Bang
Spider Women by A. Cameron
An Eskimo Birthday by T. Robinson
On Mother's Lap by A. Scott
Sharing Our Worlds by United Indians of All Tribes Foundation

Jewish Families:
I Love Hanukkah by M. Hirsh
The Rabbi and the Twenty-Nine Witches by M. Hirsh
I Am an Orthodox Jew by L. Greene

Gay/Lesbian Families:
Jenny Lives with Eric and Martin by S. Bosche
Your Family, My Family by J. Drescher

Disabilities:
Darlene by E. Greenfield
I Have a Sister, My Sister is Deaf by J. Peterson
Our Teacher is in a Wheelchair by M.E. Powers and S. Cairo
My Favorite Place by S. Sargent-Wirth
Our Brother has Down's Syndrome by S. Cairo

14. Guidance and Discipline

Each child in your program will be a little bit different; he or she will have different characteristics. More important, however, are the values and behavior patterns each child learns from his environment.

A child's attitudes about life comes from his parents, teachers, caregivers, and peers. Many children will have a happy, cheerful disposition; others will appear sad, shy, or angry. A few children suffer from separation anxiety and show their fears. On any given day, a child will display several emotions.

As the caregiver in a program, it's important to gain the trust of the parents, so you can work together, listening to parental concerns and offering suggestions for handling problems. With trust, parents will understand that you are providing a loving, enriching learning environment for their child.

Once you learn how to handle discipline problems appropriately, you will enjoy the children and your career more. Once you understand that it's better to reward good behavior than to punish bad behavior, the children will learn in a positive manner.

REWARDS

Some of the social rewards for children are: attention, smiles, praise, love, and patting. Just as you enjoy a pat on the back, children also enjoy recognition. Children also like material rewards such as gum, toys, gifts, clothes, and money.

Both kinds of rewards work. However, social rewards are always available; frequent material rewards may create more behavioral problems. (Children may refuse to behave without a material reward.)

On a daily basis, caring for children can be both rewarding and frustrating. Some days you'll have fun; other days the work will be tiring and discouraging. Usually it's a little of both.

DISCIPLINE

Discipline means setting limits that will guide and help children learn appropriate behavior. Most caregivers use one or more of the following discipline techniques:

Redirection: As a preventive technique, redirection involves planning ahead, anticipating problems, and intervening. Arrange your classroom for toy accessibility at the children's hand-eye level. With plenty of interesting toys, games, and activities, children are less likely to get into trouble.

Distraction: Distraction is one of the best devices a caregiver can use to divert a child's behavior from undesirable actions to more acceptable behavior. Change a child's focus from an unacceptable activity to one that is acceptable. For example, if a child is attempting to take a classmate's toy, give him or her another toy.

Ignoring: Ask yourself early on, "Is this a behavior I can live with in my program?" If so, ignore it. Behavior, of course, should never hurt the child himself or another child. For example, a child might dump puzzle pieces on the floor instead of on the designated activity table. As long as no one is hurt, the caregiver may choose to let the incident pass for the time being and reinforce the rules at a later time.

Time Out: "Time out" is a commonly used discipline technique when children misbehave, fight, or squabble. Set aside a special place or chair for the child to go. This gives the child a chance to calm down and realize that you will not tolerate certain types of behavior. Leave the child in the special chair or place for three to five minutes only — any longer than this and he may forget why he is there. Children have short memory spans. Match your guidance to the child's age. Behavior that is naughty for an older child may be normal for the younger child.

Some Do's and Don'ts in Behavior

DO prevent hurtful behavior by holding the child and saying, "I will not let you hurt Kevin."

DO remove a child from others for a period of time, allowing him or her to regain composure.

DO take away any object that has been used to hurt another.

DON'T force the child to say, "I'm sorry; it won't happen again." Making these statements won't make it so.

DON'T hurt or hit the child back. Hitting sets a bad example and offers a poor model for handling conflict.

DON'T threaten to like only the good children or to label a child as "bad."

Whether you're a new caregiver or an experienced one, always remember to have a sense of humor when working with children. As one child psychologist said, "You can't control what goes into a child's mouth or what comes out the other end."

Or as another writer expresses it: "Anger is like wet paint; it rubs off on everything it touches."

A FEW WORDS ABOUT CHILD ABUSE AND NEGLECT

People who enter the child care field believe that their programs are designed for the benefit of children and their families. They want to make a positive contribution to society. In turn, children and their parents expect child caregivers to meet each child's physical, emotional, social, and intellectual needs, and rightfully so. However, caregivers, much like parents, sometimes make mistakes. And because caregivers have their own needs and problems, they don't always do what's best for children.

When the media focuses on such cases as the McMartins, parents and the public take a sudden interest in day care programs. The stories create sensationalism, but in reality less than two percent of today's child abuse occurs in day care programs.

Most abuse occurs in the child's home. Thankfully, the majority of child care programs provide safe havens for children. In fact, many states have an agreement with the Department of Social Services to pay for child care, as part of a family treatment program for children from abusive families. There are few better places than safe, warm, nurturing child care centers for children who are at high risk for abuse. As a child care provider, you may play a key role in keeping families together.

A Closer Look at the Child Care Provider's Positive Role

As a child care provider, you can play several positive roles:
- You will become a role model for the children you care for as well as for their parents, many of whom are unprepared to be parents.
- Through your child care programs, you can help parents build warm relationships with other adults and children.
- Because you have daily contact with parents and children, you may be the first to notice that a family is in crisis or that a child is at risk for child abuse. Early intervention may save a child from harm or abuse.
- You can help parents build reasonable expectations for their children by creating an environment that offers age-appropriate activities.
- You can help parents understand that all children in certain stages of development will have certain annoying behaviors.

Reporting Child Abuse

As a caregiver in your home or in a day care program, you are in the position to observe inappropriate parenting styles. You may observe parents who try to control their children by hitting them or emotionally damaging them. Because children are vulnerable and usually cannot speak for themselves, they need protection. State laws provide the legal basis for action and intervention by public agencies when a child is maltreated.

You'll first have to assess the situation, taking into consideration the best interests of the child. Children have a right to love, safety, good nutrition, and physical protection.

In suspected child abuse cases, you will have to consider your own moral and legal responsibilities. In most states, people who work directly with children are considered mandated reporters.

Use your professional training, experience, and knowledge of the family before making a decision about reporting abuse. You are protected by law when you report in good faith what you believe to be child abuse or neglect. Unfortunately, child abuse and neglect are the leading causes of death among children under five years of age in the United States.

A telephone call must be made to a child protection agency when there is suspicion of physical or sexual abuse. In most states you will call the Department of Social Services or your local police department. Some agencies have special toll-free hot lines for handling cases of child abuse.

Defining Child Abuse

The following signs and patterns may indicate child abuse:

Physical Abuse:
Appearance
Unusual bruises, welts, burns, or fractures
Bite marks
Frequent injuries, always explained as accidental
Inappropriate clothing for the weather such as a long-sleeved jacket in warm weather

Behavior
Child states injury was caused by parent
Displays anti-social behavior with other children and adults
Appears frightened of parents
Avoids physical contact with adults

Emotional Abuse:
Behavior
Withdrawn, depressed
Makes comments such as, "Daddy says I'm bad."
No verbal or physical communication with others
Considered a behavior problem
Unusually shy; too submissive or anxious to please
Always pestering others; hard to get along with
Either too adult or overly young in their actions

Sexual Abuse:
Appearance
Wearing torn, stained, or bloody underclothing
Tearing, bruising, or inflammation of mouth, anus, or genitals; evidence of semen
Has venereal disease

Behavior
Talks about being sexually abused
Shows early or unusual awareness of sex
Shows delinquent tendencies or runs away

Neglect:
Appearance
Dirty, tired, non-energetic
Hasn't had breakfast; no lunch or lunch money
Needs glasses, dental care, or other medical attention

Behavior
Frequently misses school
Begs for or steals food
Spends long periods of time alone

For more information on child abuse referral agencies, contact:
CHILD HELP USA
P.O. Box 630
Hollywood, CA 90028
(800) 422-4453

APPENDICES

1. Professional Organizations and Advocacy Groups
2. Journals, Newsletters, and Periodicals

1. Professional Organizations and Advocacy Groups

Take time to become familiar with professional organizations and advocacy groups so you can make the best possible career decision. These groups usually have conferences, where you will have a chance to network with others in the field. Many times job positions are posted, and you can obtain information about the group's periodicals, newsletters, and membership.

ASSOCIATION FOR CHILDHOOD EDUCATION INTERNATIONAL (ACEI)
11141 Georgia Ave., Suite 200
Wheaton, MD 20902
(301) 942-2443

ACEI is an international child care organization interested in promoting good educational practices for children from infancy to adolescence.

ASSOCIATION FOR THE CARE OF CHILDREN'S HEALTH (ACCH)
Child Life Council
3615 Wisconsin Ave. NW
Washington, DC 20007
(202) 966-7300

This interdisciplinary international association promotes psychosocial health care for children and families in health care settings. A membership organization, it provides a job bank and publications.

CHILD CARE ACTION CAMPAIGN
330 7th Ave., 18th Floor
New York, NY 10001
(212) 239-0138

This group is a coalition of leaders from a wide range of organizations who have joined together to inform the public about the nation's child care crisis and the possible solutions.

CHILD CARE EMPLOYEE PROJECT (CCEP)
6536 Telegraph Ave., Suite A201
Oakland, CA 94609
(415) 653-9889

CCEP is a non-profit advocacy organization working to improve the wages, status, and working conditions of the child care profession. It provides information on staffing, substitute teachers, break policies, and unionizing. In 1989, the organization completed the National Child Care Staffing Study.

CHILD CARE LAW CENTER
22 Second St., 5th Floor
San Francisco, CA 94105
(415) 495-5498

This group provides legal representation for non-profit child care programs and family child care providers. It also provides technical assistance on legislation at local, state, and federal levels and public education through presentations and publications.

CHILD DEVELOPMENT ASSOCIATE
National Credentialing Program
1718 Connecticut Ave. NW, Suite 500
Washington, DC 20009
(800) 424-4310

This is a competency-based credential based on the child care provider's work with children, staff, and parents. Family day care providers and employees of day care centers may apply.

CHILD WELFARE LEAGUE OF AMERICA (CWLA)
440 1st St. NW
Washington, DC 20001-2085
(202) 638-2952

This is the oldest (founded in 1920) and largest voluntary membership organization devoted entirely to protecting and promoting the well-being of children. CWLA produces more than 100 publications, including four newsletters on public policy and legislation.

CHILDREN NOW
1913 14th St.
Santa Monica, CA 90404
(213) 470-2333

A non-partisan statewide organization, Children Now's mission is to improve the lives of California's children through policy development, legislation, education, and the media, with special attention focused on children and families who are poor or at risk.

CHILDREN'S ADVOCACY INSTITUTE
926 J St., Suite 709
Sacramento, CA 95814
(916) 444-3875

This non-profit public interest organization is dedicated to promoting the well-being of children in California. CAI currently focuses on improving child abuse intervention and prevention systems, increasing the quality and quantity of child care, and restructuring the organization of the state's delivery of children's services.

CHILDREN'S DEFENSE FUND
122 C St. NW
Washington, DC 20001
(202) 628-8787

A private non-profit organization, this group provides a strong and effective voice for the children of America. Their goal is to educate the nation about the needs of children and encourage preventive investment in children's programs, with special emphasis on poor, minority, and disabled children. The organization also spearheaded efforts to ensure the passage of the Child Care Development Grant Bill, which was passed in 1990.

CHILDREN'S FOUNDATION
815 1st St. NW, Suite 928
Washington, DC 20005
(202) 347-3300

This organization supports family day care providers with resources, advice, and its National Family Day Care Advocacy Project.

E.R.I.C.
College of Education, University of Illinois
805 W. Pennsylvania Ave.
Urbana, IL 61801
(217) 333-1386

E.R.I.C. is a clearinghouse on early childhood and elementary education materials. It maintains computer lists of every available article and manuscript on child care, child development, and child education.

INTERNATIONAL NANNY ASSOCIATION (INA)
975 N. Foothill Blvd., Suite 591
Claremont, CA 91711
(714) 622-6303

The International Nanny Association is a private, non-profit organization that serves as an advocacy group and information clearinghouse for those participating in the nanny profession and those involved in the education, placement, and employment of professionally trained nannies and in-home child care specialists.

NATIONAL ASSOCIATION FOR THE EDUCATION OF YOUNG
    CHILDREN (NAEYC)
1834 Connecticut Ave. NW
Washington, DC 20009-5786
(800) 424-2460

With more than 74,000 members, NAEYC is the nation's largest membership organization of early childhood professionals and others dedicated to improving the quality of services for young children and their families. It offers a wide range of services to assist early childhood professionals, parents, and policymakers.

NATIONAL ASSOCIATION FOR FAMILY DAY CARE (NAFDC)
815 15th St. NW, Suite 928
Washington, DC 20005
(202) 347-3356

Founded by and designed for family day care providers, NAFDC promotes the quality of family child care, eliminates isolation among providers, and acts as advocate for public policy changes.

NATIONAL BLACK CHILD DEVELOPMENT INSTITUTE
1463 Rhode Island Ave. NW
Washington, DC 20005
(202) 387-1281

The NBCDI is a non-profit, charitable organization dedicated to improving the quality of life for Black children and their families. It focuses primarily on issues and services pertaining to health, child welfare, education, and child care/early childhood education.

NATIONAL COUNCIL OF JEWISH WOMEN
53 West 23rd St.
New York, NY 10010
(212) 645-4048

With a national membership of 100,000, this organization has a history of community service and advocacy. It conducts the National Family Day Care Project, a three-year initiative to pioneer effective roles for volunteers in supporting providers at the grassroots level in thirty communities across the country.

RESOURCES FOR CHILDCARING
Toys 'N Things Press
450 N. Syndicate St., Suite 5
St. Paul, MN 55104-4227
(800) 423-8309

This non-profit organization provides a variety of services designed to improve the quality of care for young children. It publishes and distributes a wide selection of materials for child care providers.

RESULTS
236 Massachusetts Ave. NE, Suite 300
Washington, DC 20002
(202) 543-9340

Advocates for the passage of the Universal Childhood Security Act of 1990, Results is an international, grassroots citizens' lobby. In September 1990, the group sponsored the Children's Summit at the United Nations, where more than seventy heads of nations attended.

SAVE THE CHILDREN CHILD CARE SUPPORT CENTER
1340 Spring St. NW, Suite 200
Atlanta, GA 30309
(404) 885-1578

This organization offers technical assistance to family day care providers and day care centers. It sponsors an annual Family Day Care Technical Assistance Conference.

SCHOOL AGE CHILD CARE PROJECT
Center for Research on Women
Wellesley College, Cheever House
Wellesley, MA 02181
(617) 234-0320

This valuable resource is a clearinghouse providing technical assistance in establishing school-age child care.

2. Journals, Newsletters, and Periodicals

Most of the multitude of diverse groups involved in the child care field publish journals, newsletters, or periodicals. Please call or write the listings for information about subscription rates.

Legislative and Advocacy Interests

Children's Defense Reports
Children's Defense Fund
122 C St. NW, Suite 928
Washington, DC 20001
(202) 628-8787

This monthly newsletter emphasizes the needs of America's poor, minority, and handicapped children.

Directors/Administrators

Child Care Information Exchange
P.O. Box 2890
Redmond, WA 98073-2890
(206) 883-9394

This bimonthly magazine provides an in-depth focus on planning, recruiting, hiring staff, health, safety, and money management.

Center Management
Engle Communication Inc.
820 Bear Tavern Rd.
West Trenton, NJ 08628
(609) 530-0044

Published monthly except July/August and December/January, this publication focuses on such issues as management, corporate relations, cost of child care, and designing centers.

Child Care Workers' Rights

Child Care Employee News
6536 Telegraph Ave., Suite A-201
Oakland, CA 94609

Published quarterly, this advocacy publication is dedicated to improving child care through better wages and working conditions.

Child Development Interests

Beginnings
P.O. Box 2890
Redmond, WA 98052
(206) 883-9394

This quarterly publication provides an in-depth focus on infant and toddler stages of development and activities for this age group.

School Age Notes
P.O. Box 120674
Nashville, TN 37212
(615) 292-2957

Published six times a year, this publication focuses on those who care for the school-age child.

High/Scope® Resource
600 N. River St.
Ypsilanti, MI 48198-2898
(313) 485-2000

Published three times a year, this publication provides a guide to the activities, products, and services of the High/Scope® Foundation.

Young Children
National Association for the Education of Young Children
1834 Connecticut Ave. NW
Washington, DC 20009
(800) 424-2460

A bimonthly journal, this publication offers information on early childhood research, theory, and practice.

Nannies

Nanny Times
Jack and Jill Enterprises, Inc.
P.O. Box 31
Rutherford, NJ 07070
(201) 935-5575

National Nanny Newsletter
976 W. Foothill Blvd., Suite 591
Claremont, CA 91711
(714) 622-6303

Family Day Care

Family Daycare Exchange of Information and Ideas
Cooperative Extension Service
Iowa State University
Ames, IA 50011

This excellent newsletter series focuses on health and safety, guidance and discipline, and child development issues.

Caring—Information for Family Day Care Providers
ANR Publications
Cooperative Extension
Univ. of California Div. of Agriculture & Natural Resources
6701 San Pablo Ave.
Oakland, CA 94608-1239
(415) 642-2431

This publication may be ordered as individual copies or as a complete series. The information includes language development, meals and snacks, and business uses of the home.

Family Day Care Caring
Toys 'N Things Press
450 N. Syndicate St., Suite 5
St. Paul, MN 55104-4127
(800) 423-8309

This bimonthly national magazine gives family day care providers and advocates some of the most current information, support, and resources available in the field.

The National Perspective
815 15th St. NW, Suite 928
Washington, DC 20005
(202) 347-3356

This bimonthly newsletter is a publication of the National Association for Family Day Care (NAFDC).

CCR&R Issues
The National Association of Child Care Resource & Referral Agencies
2116 Campus Dr. SE
Rochester, MN 55904
(507) 287-2020

This quarterly newsletter is available either through membership in the organization or by subscription.

Pomona Child Care Information Service
Pomona Unified School District
Child Development Programs
153 E. Pasadena St.
Pomona, CA 91767
(714) 629-5011

The author of this book is employed in this CCR&R program, and she will gladly send you a free issue of their newsletter.

GLOSSARY

AA DEGREE—Associated Arts degree conferred by community colleges after completion of required and elected courses totaling 60 semester units of study.

AFDC—Aid to Families with Dependent Children. A federal and state funded welfare program which grants funds to low income parents. Some states offer subsidized child care.

AIDE—A person who assists professional teachers or child caregivers.

ALTERNATIVE PROGRAM—A California subsidized program designed for low income families. Parents, both working and school-attending, have a choice in choosing the day care setting for their child.

BA DEGREE—Bachelor of Arts degree conferred by a four-year college or university after completion of required and elected courses totaling 120 semester units of study.

BEH—Bureau of Education for the Handicapped; now called Office of Special Education, the Department of Education.

CCR&R — Child Care Resource and Referral. These programs assist families in the selection of quality child care. They document and articulate child care and family needs to parents, child care providers, and the community. These multi-faceted programs keep data on the supply of child care and technical assistance to family day care and day care centers.

CDA — Child Development Associate. An entry level credential recognized by more than forty states.

CHILD CARE—Caring for children from birth to twelve years of age in a family day care setting or child care center to foster the child's social, emotional, physical, and intellectual needs.

CHILDREN'S CENTERS — A California subsidized program providing child care for low income families who are working in training programs. Children from birth to age thirteen who are abused, neglected, or at risk receive the highest priority for these services.

COGNITION—The mental process of gaining knowledge.

COOPERATIVE NURSERY SCHOOL — A non-profit nursery school program, managed and staffed by parents with a hired teacher or director.

CPSW—Child Protection Social Worker.

CURRICULUM—A set of planned program activities designed to foster the child's development.

DAY CARE CENTER—A facility designed for the care of children in a particular age group, including infants to twelve years of age. Usually open 10 to 12 hours a day.

ECE—Early Childhood Education.

EHA—Education of the Handicapped Act.

EXTENDED DAY CARE PROGRAMS — Sometimes called "before and after school child care," this program is for the school-age child. They are usually located on school district sites, in day care centers, in family day care homes, or are administered by the "Y" or parks and recreations programs.

FAMILY DAY CARE—Home child care for children who are unrelated to the provider. Licensing is usually for six or fewer children. Income is derived from parental fees or voucher payments from government subsidies.

FGP—Foster Grandparent Program.

HEAD START—A national federally-sponsored program started in 1965 to give children from lower-income families a head start in preparing for school. This comprehensive program provides education, health, nutrition, and social services to four year olds.

HIGH/SCOPE® — A curriculum designed to use the "plan and do review" method.

HOSPITAL CHILD CARE—Usually performed by a child life specialist, these child care or educational services are provided in a hospital setting.

INFANT — The term given to a child from birth to approximately eighteen months or up until the child begins to walk.

INFANT DAY CENTER — A day care program designed for children under 2½ years of age. It may be part of a larger center or a separate program. Usually, there are two caregivers for every eight children.

KINDERGARTEN — A public or private educational program for children ages 4½ to 5 years. Usually a three-hour program.

LABORATORY SCHOOL—A special school within a community college or university offering a lab for students to practice teaching and caring for preschool children.

LICENSED FACILITY—Each state sets minimum standards, including child safety and health protection, for licensing day care centers or family day care homes.

MINIMUM WAGE—As of April 1, 1991, the federal minimum wage was set at $4.25.

MONTESSORI SCHOOLS—A special education program based on the philosophy originally developed by Maria Montessori.

NANNY—A person hired to provide live-in or live-out care for a child in his or her home. In addition to salaries, live-in nannies receive room and board.

NURSERY SCHOOL—These schools started in the 1930's to provide part-time, morning or afternoon, programs for preschool age children. The term remains today for many of the older schools and programs.

PRESCHOOL—Has the same concept as a nursery school, offering part-time programs for preschoolers ages 2½ to 5.

PROPRIETARY DAY CARE — These centers are privately-owned and managed on a for-profit basis.

SIDS—Sudden Infant Death Syndrome, sometimes called crib death.

VENDOR VOUCHERS—Refers to a specific form of payment for child care programs. The agency who issues these payments may pay the provider directly (vendor). Other agencies pay cash payments to the parent directly (voucher). Employees may redeem a voucher for child care services.

SUGGESTED READING

Baden, Ruth K. and others. *School-Age Child Care: An Action Manual*, Auburn House Publishing Co., Boston, MA, 1982.

Baker, Katherine. *The Nursery School*, Human Relations and Learning, W.B. Saunders Company.

Bender, Judith and others. *Half a Childhood*, School Age Notes, Nashville, TN, 1984.

Blau, R. and others. *Activities for School-Age Child Care*, NAEYC, Washington, DC.

Carmichael, Viola S. *Science Experiences for Young Children*, SCAEYC, Los Angeles, CA, 1974.

Cherry, Clare. *Creative Art for the Developing Child*, Fearon Publishing, Belmont, CA.

Cherry, Clare. *Creative Movement for the Developing Child*, Fearon Publishing, Belmont, CA.

Deery, Patty and Cindy Ham. *Helping Baby Grow*, T.S. Denison & Company, Inc., Minneapolis, MN, 1989.

Fraiberg, Selma H. *The Magic Years*, Charles Scribner's Sons, New York, NY, 1959.

Elkind, David, *The Hurried Child*, Addison-Wesley, Menlo Park, CA, 1983.

Evans, Judith and Ellen Ilfeld. *Good Beginnings*, The High/Scope Press, Ypsilanti, MI.

Galinsky, Ellen and Judy David. *The Preschool Years*, Times Books, New York, NY, 1988.

Gerber, M. *Resources for Infant Educarers*, Los Angeles 1981.

Greenfield, Patricia Marks and Edward Tronick. *Infant Curriculum*, Goodyear Publishing Company, Inc., Santa Monica, CA, 1980.

Klaus, Marshall H. and Phyllis H. Klaus. *The Amazing Newborn*, Addison-Wesley Publishing Company, Inc., New York, NY, 1985.

Lally, J.R. and I. Gordon. *Learning Games for Infants and Toddlers*, Non-Readers Press, Syracuse, NY, 1977.

Leach, Penelope. *Your Baby and Child*. Alfred A. Knopf, New York, NY, 1987.

Maynard, Fredelle. *The Child Care Crisis*, Penguin Books Canada Limited, Markham, Ontario, Canada, 1985.

Miller, Karen. *Things to Do with Toddlers and Twos*, Telshare Publishing Co., Inc., Marshfield, MA, 1984.

Muscari, Ann and Wenda Morrone. *Child Care That Works*, Doubleday,

New York, NY, 1989.

Neugebauer, Roger. "School Age Day Care," Care Information Exchange (Reprint: 101), Redmond, WA.

Schrank, Rita. *Toddlers Learn by Doing*, Humanics Limited, Atlanta, GA, 1984.

Segal, Marty and Dan Adcroft. *A Child at Play. One to Two Years*, Newmarket Press, New York, NY, 1985.

White, Burton L. *The First Three Years of Life*. Avon Books, New York, NY, 1978.

BIBLIOGRAPHY

Anzalone, Joan, editor. *Good Works: A Guide to Careers in Social Change*, Dembner Books, New York, 1985.

Bellm, Dan. *Making A Difference*, California Child Care Resource and Referral Network, San Francisco, CA, 1987.

Bellm, Dan and others. *Family Day Care Handbook*, California Day Child Care Resource and Referral Network, San Francisco, CA, 1988.

Burud, L. Sandra and Cynthia Ransom. *Directory of Corporate Child Care Assistance Programs*, Burud & Associates, Pasadena, CA, 1988.

California State Department of Education. *Program Facts 1988*, Sacramento, CA, 1988.

Child Care Employee Project. *Working for Quality Child Care*, Child Care Employee Project, Berkeley, CA, 1989.

----. *The National Child Care Staffing Study*, Child Care Employee Project, Berkeley, CA, 1989.

Children's Defense Fund. *Children 1990: A Report Card, Briefing and Action Primer*, National Association for the Education of Young Children, Washington, DC, 1990.

Click, Phyllis. *Administration of Schools for Young Children*, Delmar Publishers Inc., Albany, NY, 1981.

Decker, Celia Anita and John R. Decker. *Planning and Administering Early Childhood Programs*, Merrill Publishing Company, Columbus, OH, 1988.

Derman-Sparks, Louise and the A.B.C. Task Force. *Anti-Bias Curriculum*, NAEYC, Washington, DC, 1989.

Dorman, Pat. *History of Child Care/Preschool, On the Capitol Door Step*, Sacramento, CA, 1988.

Ewing, Bill. From an unpublished paper. Copyrighted 1986.

Feeney, Stephanie and others. *Who Am I in the Lives of Children?* Merrill Publishing Company, Columbus, OH, 1987.

Ford Foundation Project on Social Welfare and the American Future. *The Common Good: Social Welfare and the American Future*, Ford Foundation, New York, 1989.

Garcia, Rhoda. *Designing a Family Day Care Program—Home Centered Care*, Children Council of San Francisco, CA, 1985.

Hanft, Barbara E., editor. *Family-Centered Care: Early Intervention Resource Manual*, The American Occupational Therapy Association, Rockville, MD, 1989.

Ispa, Jean. *Exploring Careers in Child Care Services*, The Rosen Publishing Group, Inc., New York, 1984.

Los Angeles Roundtable for Children. *Services for Children with Disabilities in Los Angeles County*, Los Angeles, 1988.

Marhoefer, Patricia E. and Lisa A. Vadnais. *Caring for the Developing Child*, Delmar Publishers, Inc., Albany, NY, 1988

Morgan, Gwen. *The National State of Child Care Regulations 1986*, Work Family Directions, Boston, MA, 1987.

Mullin-Rindler, Nancy and Susan Twombly. *Child Care Resource & Referral. Counselors & Trainers Manual*, Toys 'n Things Press, St. Paul, MN, 1989.

NAEYC. *The Child Care Boom. Growth in Licensed Child Care from 1977 to 1985*, NAEYC, Washington, DC, 1985.

----. *In Whose Hands? A Demographic Fact Sheet on Child Care Providers*, NAEYC, Washington, DC, 1985.

----. *Careers in ECE*, NAEYC, Washington, DC, 1987.

----. "Public Policy Reports Young Children," NAEYC, Washington, DC, 1990.

Neugebauer, Roger. "Surveying the Landscape: A Look at Child Care '89," Child Care Information Exchange, Redmond, WA, April 1989.

Nicoll, Dr. Barbara J. "The Pasadena/San Gabriel Valley Early Childhood Salary Survey: 1989."

Phillips Brunson, Carol. "The Child Development Associate Program, Young Children," NAEYC, Washington, DC, March 1990.

Sanders, Judy. "Synopsis of High/Scope Introduction," 1989.

Seaver, J.W. and others. *Careers with Young Children: Making Your Decision*, NAEYC, Washington, DC, 1979.

Siegel, Patricia and Lawrence Merle. "Developing Child Care Resource and Referral Services," California Child Care Resource and Referral Network, San Francisco, CA, 1982.

Struntz, Karen A. and Shari Reville. *Growing Together: An Intergenerational Source Book*, The American Society of Retired Persons & the Elvirita Lewis Foundation, Washington, DC, 1985.

U.S. Department of Health and Human Services. *Head Start and Child Development Program*, Washington, DC, 1986.

U.S. Department of Labor, Bureau of Labor Statistics. *Occupational Outlook 1988*, Washington, DC, 1988.

U.S. Secretary Task Force. "Child Care Work Force," Issue, 1988.

Whitebook, Marcy and Debra Phillip. "Who are Child Care Workers?" Journal: *Young Children*, NAEYC, Washington, DC, 1986.

Wittenberg, Renee. *Opportunities in Child Care Careers*, VGM Career Horizons, Lincolnwood, IL, 1988.

Index

A

AA, see Associated Arts degree
Abuse and neglect, 145-7
Act for Child Care, 52, 53
Administration of Children, Youth and Families, 52
Adoff, A., *Black is Brown is Tan*, 140
Advocacy groups, 151-5
Advocate, see Child care advocate
Alternative payment program, 56, 72, 76
Alternative payment worker, 76
American Montessori Society Inc., 43
Aristotle, 14
Art, as part of curriculum, 130-1
Associated Arts degree, 26
Association for Childhood Education International (ACEI), 151
Association for the Care of Children's Health (ACCH), 66, 151
Association Montessori International, 43
Association Montessori International U.S.A., 43
Author/illustrator, 68
Authorization for Emergency Medical Care, 83
Authorization to Administer Medication, 84

B

Bang, M., *The Paper Crane*, 141
Ten, Nine, Eight, 140
Beckley-Cardy, 68
Beginnings, 158
Behaviorist approach, 15
Bemelmans, Ludwig, *Madeline*, 134
Benefits, available in private sector jobs, 48-9
Berg, Barbara, 61
Blue, R., *I Am Here/Yo Estoy Aqui*, 141
Bood, C., *The Goat in the Rug*, 141

Bosche, S., *Jenny Lives with Eric and Martin*, 141
Broome County Intergenerational Activities Program, 112, 114
Brown, Margaret Wise, *The Noisy Book*, 134
Brummel, Steven, 112
Bureau of Education for the Handicapped, 106
Bureau of Labor Statistics, 37
Burud, Sandra, 42
Business plan, 94-5

C

Cairo, S., *Our Brother has Down's Syndrome*, 141
Our Teacher is in a Wheelchair, 141
California Child Care Resource and Referral Network, 79
California Children's Lobby, 114
California's child care system, 55-8
Cameron, A., *Spider Women*, 141
Camp counselor, 67
Careers, 13, 37-49, 59-68, 103-16
new century, 103-16
private sector, 37-49
Caring—Information for Family Day Care Providers, 159
CCR&R Issues, 159
CDA, see Child Development Associate
Center Management, 157
Cervantes, Robert, 55
Chang, K., *The Iron Moonhunter*, 141
Charles R. Drew University of Medicine and Science, 109, 110
Chavez, Caesar, 110
Child abuse and neglect, 145-7
defining, 146-7
reporting, 145-6
Child care, need for quality, 101-2
Child care, religious-related, 42-3
Child Care Action Campaign, 151
Child care advocate, 117-20

—169—

170 ■ CAREERS IN CHILD CARE

Child Care and Development Block Grant, 53, 115, 120
Child care centers, 42-3, 91-102
  budgets, 96-7
  building criteria, 93-4
  business plan, 94-5
  church-related, 42-3
  developing program, 99
  employer-related, 42
  equipment and materials, 96-7
  financial considerations, 95-6
  independent, 42
  location, 92-3
  outdoor playground, 98
  planning, 94-5
  promoting, 99-101
  regulations, 92
  responsibilities involved, 91-2
  staff, 98-9
Child care consultants, 61-2
  wages, 62
Child care coordinators, 62-3
  duties, 63
  wages, 63
Child care director, day in the life of, 45-6
Child Care Employee News, 157
Child Care Employee Project, 48-9, 117, 119, 151-2
Child Care Food Program, 73, 85-6
Child care food provider coordinator, 74-5
Child Care Information Exchange, 24, 157
Child care instructors, 63-5
  college, 63-4
  parent-child educator, 65
  vocational, 64-5
Child Care Law Center, 152
Child care lobbyist, 114-5
Child care ombudsman, 67
Child care programs, parks and recreation, 44
Child Care Resource & Referral agencies, 13, 29, 69-79, 99
  counselor/referral workers, 71
  day in the life of, 76-9
  job banks, 70-1
  job opportunities, 74-6
    alternative payment/respite worker, 76

counselor/referral specialist, 75
executive director, 75-6
food provider coordinator, 74-5
GAIN Program Specialist, 74
manager, 75
Child Care Resource & Referral resources, 79
Child Development Associate, 26-7
  competency goals, 27
Child Development Associate Consortium, 26
Child Development Associate National Credentialing Program, 152
Child development field, 13-20
Child Help USA, 147
Child life specialist, 66
Child Protection Social Worker (CPSW), 104-6
  job sites, 105
  professional organizations, 106
  qualifications of, 105
  salaries, 105-6
  types of services, 104-5
Child Welfare League of America (CWLA), 152
Childcraft, 68
Childhood and Society, 15
Children, ages and stages, 16-8
Children, eight to ten year olds, development, 19
Children, five year olds, development, 19
Children, six to eight year olds, development, 19
Children Now, 152
Children's Advocacy Institute, 152
Children's Bureau, 51
Children's Defense Fund, 115, 120, 153
Children's Defense Reports, 157
Children's Foundation, 153
Children's Services Center, 108
Children's World, 42
Church-related child care programs, 42-3
Cliffton, L., *Don't You Remember?*, 140
Cognitive approach, 14-5
Cohn, Jean, 64
College child care instructors, 63-4

Comenius, John, 14
Constant, H., *First Snow*, 141
Constructive Playthings, 68
Contracts, for family day care, 88
Cooperative preschools, 44
Council for Early Childhood Professional Recognition, 27
Council Social Work Education, 106
Counselor/referral workers, 71
Cover letter, 34
Curriculum, 123-37, 139-41
  areas of classroom focus, 130-4
  classroom environments, 136-7
  games for infants and toddlers, 124-5
  infants and toddlers, 123-4
  multicultural/anti-bias, 139-41
  activities, 140-1
  preschool, 126-7
  school-age, 135-6

D

Darwin, Charles, 14
Day care, need for quality, 101-2
Day care center, 42-3, 91-102
  budgets, 96-7
  building criteria, 93-4
  business plan, 94-5
  church-related, 42-3
  developing program, 99
  employer-related, 42
  equipment and materials, 96-7
  financial considerations, 95-6
  independent, 42
  location, 92-3
  outdoor playground, 98
  planning, 94-5
  promoting, 99-101
  regulations, 92
  staff, 98-9
De Brunhoff, Jean, *The Story of Babar*, 134
Department of Health and Human Services, 52
Department of Health, Education and Welfare, 51, 52
Dewey, John, 110
Disabled children, workers for, 106-7
Discipline, 86-7, 143-4
  rewards, 143

Dodd, Chris, 53
Drescher, J., *Your Family, My Family*, 141
Drug-exposed children, 108-10

E

E.R.I.C., 153
Early childhood administrator, 38-9
Early childhood education, 14-5, 51-2
  historical roots of, 14-5
  legislative history, 51-2
Early childhood teacher, 22-4, 39
  self-evaluation form, 22-4
Eastman, P.D., *Are You My Mother?*, 134
ECE, see Early childhood education
Edelman, Marian Wright, 120
Education of the Handicapped Act, 107
Employer-related child care services, 73-4
Employer-Supported Child Care and Directory of Corporate Child Care, 42
Erickson, Eric, 15
Evaluating personal needs, 21
Ewing, Bill, 57
Expression of the Emotions in Man and Animals, 14
Extended day care teacher, 40

F

Family day care, 81-9
  activities, 82
  advantages, 81
  business of, 87-9
  child care food program, 85-6
  contracts, 88
  disadvantages, 81-2
  discipline, 86-7
  food and nutrition, 84-5
  health, 83
  record keeping, 88-9
  recruiting children, 88
  safety, 82-3
  setting fees, 87
  taxes, 88-9
Family Day Care Association, 82
Family Day Care Caring, 159

Family Daycare Exchange of Information and Ideas, 158-9
Family Support Act of 1988, 72
Fees for family day care, 87
Food program, 73
For Love of Children (FLOC), 115
Foster Grandparent Program (FGP), 113
Foundation for the Elvirita Lewis Center, 111-2, 114
Franklin Community Action Corporation, 115
Freud, Sigmund, 15
Froebel, Frederick, 20, 110

G

Gag, Wanda, *Millions of Cats*, 134
GAIN, 72, 74
   Program Specialist, 74
Gallaudet College, 106
Garcia, Rhonda, 139
Gerber's, 42
Gesell, Arnold, 15
Gesell approach, 15
Glossary, 161-3
Goal setting, 21-2
Goldin, A., *Straight Hair, Curly Hair*, 141
Greater Avenues for Independence (GAIN), 72
Greene, L., *I Am an Orthodox Jew*, 141
Greenfield, E., *Darlene*, 141
   Honey, I Love You, 140
Guidance, 143

H

Handford, Martin, *Where's Waldo?*, 134
Head Start, 13, 52, 53-5, 57, 109
Heide, Frances, *That's What Friends are For*, 135
Heritage Foundation, 42-3
Hernandez, Velva, 41
High/Scope® Educational Research Foundation, 27-8, 53, 109
High/Scope® *Resource*, 158
Hirsh, M., *I Love Hanukkah*, 141
   The Rabbi and the Twenty-Nine Witches, 141
Historical roots of early childhood education, 14-5
   behaviorist approach, 15
   cognitive approach, 14-5
   Gesell approach, 15
   humanistic approach, 14
   psychosocial development theory, 15
Home Centered Care: Designing a Family Day Care Program, 139
Hudson, Dennis, 61
Humanistic/maturational views of early childhood education, 14
Hunter-Hamilton, Hanna, 109

I

IBM, 42
Infant-toddler teacher, 39-40
Infants, 16-7, 123-5
   curriculum for, 123-4
   games for, 124-5
   stages of development, 16-7
Intergenerational programs, 110-4
   resources for, 113-4
Internal Revenue Service, 89
International Nanny Association (INA), 153
Interview, 34-6
   of manager, 35-6
   of teacher, 34-5

J

Job, finding right, 29
Job banks, 70-1
Job opportunities, 59-68
Job-seeking techniques, 29-36
   cover letter, 34
   interview, 34-6
   résumé, 29-34
Johnston, Crockett, *The Carrot Seed*, 134
Jones, Joanna, 63-4
Journals, 157-9

K

Kaplan School Supply Corp., 68, 97
Keats, Ezra Jack, *The Snowy Day*, 134
Keeny, Sarah, 107-8
KinderCare, 41-2

L

La Petite, 41, 42
Lakeshore, 68

Language arts, as part of curriculum, 133-4
Lanham Act, 51
Latchkey teacher, 40
Lincoln, Abraham, 106
Link, M., *The Goat in the Rug*, 141
Lionni, Leo, *Swimmy*, 135
Lobbyist, 114-5
Luther, Martin, 14

M

Malaske-Samu, Kathy, 63
Management position, interviewing for, 35-6
Marhoefer, Pattie, 64
Martel, C., *Yaga Days*, 140
Math, as part of curriculum, 133
"Maturational Approach," 14
McGovern, A., *Black is Beautiful*, 140
Mead, Margaret, 111, 120
Mills College, 66
Montessori, Maria, 43, 110
Montessori schools, 43
Munsch, Robert, *Love You Forever*, 134
Music, as part of curriculum, 131-2

N

NAEYC, see National Association for the Education of Young Children
Nannies, 59-61
 duties, 60
 wages, 60-1
 working conditions, 60
Nanny Times, 158
National Association for Family Day Care (NAFDC), 154
National Association for the Education of Young Children (NAEYC), 29, 38, 52, 82, 118-9, 153
National Association of Child Care Resource and Referral Agencies, 71, 79
National Association of Social Workers, 106
National Black Child Development Institute, 154
National chain child care organizations, 41-2
National Child Care Staffing Study, 48, 117, 119
National Council of Jewish Women, 154
National Federation of Day Nurseries, 51
National Nanny Newsletter, 158
National Perspective, The, 159
National SIDS Foundation, 84
National State of Child Care Regulations, 39, 40
Neglect, of child, 145-7
Newsletters, 157-9
Nicholls, Barbara, 49

O

Office of Child Development, 52
Office of Special Education, 106
Ombudsman, 67
Organizations, 151-5

P

Parent-child educator, 65
Parks and recreation child care programs, 44
Partnership Group, Inc., 71, 73
Pediatric rehabilitation services, 107-8
 positions, 108
Periodicals, 157-9
Pestalozi, Johann H., 14
Peterson, J., *I Have a Sister, My Sister is Deaf*, 141
Piaget, Jean, 15
Piper, Watty, *The Little Engine That Could*, 135
Planned Parenthood Federation of America, Inc., 116
Plato, 14
Play, importance to development of preschoolers, 19-20
Playground worker, 66
Pomona Child Care Information Service, 159
Powers, M.E., *Our Teacher is in a Wheelchair*, 141
Preschool teacher, 40, 46-7, 48
 day in the life of, 46-7
 eight-hour schedule, 48
Preschoolers, 17-8, 19-20, 125-30
 curriculum for, 126-7
 growth and development, 125-6
 how they learn, 127-30
 importance of play in development, 19-20
 stages of development, 17-8, 19

174 ■ CAREERS IN CHILD CARE

Preschools, cooperative, 44
Preschools, private, 45
Private sector careers, 37-49
  benefits, 48-9
  early childhood administrator, 38-9
  early childhood teacher, 39
  extended day care teacher, 40
  infant-toddler teacher, 39-40
  preschool teacher, 40
  salaries, 48-9
  teacher aide, 41
  types of programs, 41-5
    cooperative preschools, 44
    employer-related child care centers, 42
    independent centers, 42
    Montessori schools, 43
    national chains, 41-2
    parks and recreation, 44
    private preschool, 45
    regional chains, 42
    religious-related, 42-3
    YMCA extended day care, 44
Psychosocial development theory, 15
Public Law 91-230, 107
Public Law 94-142, 65, 107
Public Law 99-457, 107
Public sector jobs, 51-8

R

Résumé, 29-34
  format, 31-3
    chronological, 33
    functional, 32
Regional chain child care organizations, 42
Resources for Childcaring, 154
Respite care program, 56, 72, 76
  worker, 76
Results, 154
Retired Senior Volunteer Programs Action Agency, 113
Rewards, 143
Rey, H.A., *Curious George*, 134
Robinson, T., *An Eskimo Birthday*, 141
Rosenberg, M., *Living in Two Worlds*, 140
Rousseau, Jean, 14

S

Salaries, private sector, 48-9
Sales representative, 67-8
Sargent-Wirth, S., *My Favorite Place*, 141
Save the Children Child Care Support Center, 154-5
School-age child, curriculum for, 135-6
School Age Child Care Project, 155
School Age Notes, 158
Science, as part of curriculum, 132-3
SCORE, 94
Scott, A., *On Mother's Lap*, 141
Self-Evaluation for the Early Childhood Teacher, 22-4
Sendak, Maurice, *Where the Wild Things Are*, 134
Seuss, Dr., *The Cat in the Hat*, 134
Showers, P., *Listening Walk*, 129
SIDS, see Sudden Infant Death Syndrome
Simon, N., *What Do I Do? Que Hago*, 141
Skelly, Sherry, 114
Slobodkina, Esthyl, *Caps for Sale*, 134
Small Business Administration, 94, 95
Sonneborn, R., *Friday Night is Paps Night*, 141
Southern California Association for the Education of Young Children, 49
Special education teacher, 65
Special needs children, workers for, 106-7
Stoller, Dora Keyser, 110
Sudden Infant Death Syndrome, 84
Summary of Child Care Center Salaries, Benefits and Working Conditions, 48

T

Taxes, for family day care, 88-9
Teacher, interviewing for position as, 34-5
Teacher aide, 41
Teacher assistant, 41
Teacher's training programs, 25-8
  Associated Arts degree, 26

Teacher's training programs, cont.
　Child Development Associate, 26-7
　college course work, 25
　High/Scope® Educational Research Foundation, 27-8
　two-year associate, 25-6
Toddlers, 17, 18, 124-5
　curriculum for, 124
　games for, 124-5
　stages of development, 17, 18
Toys 'N Things Press, 88, 89, 154
Training programs, 25-8
　Associated Arts degree, 26
　Child Development Associate, 26-7
　college course work, 25
　High/Scope® Educational Research Foundation, 27-8
　two-year associate, 25-6
Trendwatcher Panel, 41

U
United Communities Against Poverty, 115
United Indians of All Tribes Foundation, *Sharing Our Worlds*, 141

University of Laverne, 66

V
Values, 24
Van Clief, Sylvia, *That's What Friends are For*, 135
Vocational instructors, 64-5
Voucher program, 56, 72

W
"Whole Child Approach," 14
Work/Family Directions, Inc., 71, 73
Works Progress Administration, 51

X
Xerox, 42

Y
Yashima, T., *Umbrella*, 141
YMCA extended day care programs, 44
YMCA of USA, 44
Young Children, 158

Z
Zale Jewelers, 42